MODERN PUBLIC SPEAKING

THE DEFINITIVE GUIDE TO ENGAGING AUDIENCES ONLINE AND IN-PERSON

GRANT MORGAN

INTRODUCTION

In an era where communication transcends physical boundaries and digital platforms have become as essential as traditional stages, mastering the art of public speaking has never been more crucial. "**Modern Public Speaking**: The Definitive Guide to Engaging Audiences Online and In-Person" serves as an indispensable resource for anyone looking to captivate, inform, and inspire audiences, regardless of the setting.

Public speaking is not merely about conveying information; it is about creating a connection and fostering an environment where ideas can flourish. This book delves into the nuanced techniques that enable speakers to engage effectively with their audience, whether they are in a packed auditorium or participating in a virtual conference. It explores the dynamic interplay between speaker and listener, highlighting the importance of authenticity, empathy, and adaptability.

In today's fast-paced world, speakers must navigate diverse challenges, from crafting compelling narratives to utilizing technology seamlessly. This guide provides insights into harnessing the power of storytelling, developing a commanding presence, and leveraging multimedia tools to enhance presentations. It also addresses the unique demands of online speaking, offering strategies to maintain audience interest and interaction across digital platforms.

The book is structured to benefit speakers at all levels, from novices seeking to overcome stage fright to seasoned professionals looking to refine their skills. Each chapter offers practical advice, real-world examples, and exercises designed to build confidence and competence. By blending traditional techniques with innovative approaches, "Modern Public

Speaking" equips readers with the knowledge to thrive in any speaking environment.

Ultimately, this guide is about empowering individuals to express their ideas with clarity and conviction, transforming public speaking from a daunting task into an opportunity for impactful communication. Whether addressing a live audience or engaging with viewers online, readers will find the tools they need to become persuasive, effective speakers in today's interconnected world.

Table of Contents

GRANT MORGAN

MODERN PUBLIC
SPEAKING

CHAPTER 1

The Art of Oratory

UNDERSTANDING ORATORY

Public speaking, which is sometimes fearful and often held in the highest regard, is an art that has molded the history of the world. It is a style and precise use of words, rhythm, and gestures that attract a lot of attention and motivate new things. Essentially, oratory is not simply a speech in front of a crowd but the eloquent expression of thought, feelings, and will, which turns words into eloquence.

In order to have a deeper understanding of what it takes to be a good speaker, one should first of all be able to understand the fine balance between a speaker, a message, and an audience. The speaker is the conduit of information, as he or she has a responsibility to deliver relevant information that will be appealing. This does not merely involve expertise in language, but in people, what motivates them, and what arouses their enthusiasm and feelings as well as action. This gives the basics of effective oratory based on the presence, tone, and demeanor of the speaker.

What is also key is the message. Oratory lives on the spirit of clarity and purpose. A good message can be compared to a sharpened blade that needs to cut through the noise and strike at the core of the audience. It must be consistent, well organized, and well presented. The messenger must be able to make the audience feel the message, that they are concerned with questions it evokes about the values and beliefs shared by the speaker and the audience, and that a bond of understanding exists between them.

Nevertheless, an audience is the most crucial element of oratory. Every listener contributes their views, experience, and feelings to the communication. The expert speaker is aware of such diversity and makes every effort to appeal to the audience on a personal note. This includes room awareness, sensing audience reactions, and adjusting delivery to keep the readers interested. The audience does not merely act as an abducted receiver of the message. Still, as active participant in the exchange process, they modify the progress and the effect of the message.

Oratory is a very complex undertaking, and a study of oratory would demand the endowment of inherent ability coupled with nurtured skill. It needs an immoderate mixture of belief and decrease, force and pity. The speaker has to be self-aware and have knowledge of what he or she is good at and what he or she is not, practicing their oratory and reflecting on it. The journey to this self-improvement can be characterized by being capable of listening, learning, and growing to make sure that each speech is more significant than the previous one.

Besides, the historical background of oratory enhances its impact. Whether it is the rhetorical styles of ancient Greek philosophies or modern ideologies of influential leaders, the power of speech has been instrumental in causing a change in society. It can bring people together or set them apart; it can create or destroy. It is, thus, the task of the orator not merely to his audience, but to society.

When one dives deeper into the intricacies of oratory, it is possible to adore its transformative potential. It is an ever-changing power going beyond a word spoken, the power of making people express their visions and raising people around them. Oratory, just like any other component of effective communication, is an essential undertaking in pursuit of achievement by an individual, whatever the circumstance may be in modern times of communication power in our world. The ancient art of oratory is timeless, and we look forward to every fresh generation adding something to its heritage and working out the destiny of the world by means of the living word.

The Evolution of Public Speaking

The art of public speaking, an ancient art, has its way into the history of humanity, evolving in depth and breadth with the change in society. From the first meetings around the crackling fire of the ancient hearth to the busy marketplaces of the modern meetings, art has been accepted to fit the redefining necessities of human communication.

The oral word was a potent means of conveying knowledge and culture in the ancient world; it could be the main source of that knowledge. Ancient Greece orators like Demosthenes and Cicero established the cornerstones of rhetoric, and they shaped systems and strategies that will continue to guide speakers in the next centuries. They performed to activate and stimulate the audience with their speeches, which were not only persuasions but performances. The Square of Athens and the floors of the Senate within Rome were the arenas where the art of public discourse was refined and glorified.

The medium of speech during the Middle Ages started to dominate, with religious sermons and royal declarations encompassing the use of the spoken word to evoke an idea of faith and loyalty. The pulpit of a church and the court of a monarch were the stage where domination and eloquence were blended to set down the history of nations and gave moral direction to the societies. It was during the same time that people spoke publicly not to express themselves, but to strengthen communal values and hierarchies.

The Renaissance marked a rebirth of interest in classical rhetoric, and it was combined with the common ideas of the time. This period marked the growth of the use of public speaking since they also started assuming educational, political, and aesthetic roles. The printing press also transformed the art of communication as speeches could be heard by other people outside the immediate audience, and the words could be written on paper, which made them immortal in some sense.

The Enlightenment ushered in an eagerness for reason and individualism, and so transformed the political arena of public speaking to promote the ideas and philosophize on them. Intellectuals and revolutionaries would use words to question what was established in the salons and coffeehouses of the world, as movements later arose to transform nations. Oratory speeches became a driving force of change, and such people as Voltaire and Thomas Paine would use their skills at oration to influence and ponder.

With the dawn of a modernized world, technology harnessed further finer changes to the technography of public speaking. Through radio and television, people say voices over huge distances and would make orators household names. New online channels provided a place where political leaders, entertainers, and activists could reach out to audiences that they never would have been able to do previously. The effectiveness of the speech delivered was intensified as they could now foment movements in various parts of the world or unify diverse communities.

The development of the art of public speaking has taken a new height in the digital age. Social media and internet-based media have democratized the platform, and it is now usable by all voices, even in the far reaches of the earth. The new stage has been created as a virtual stage, and people have been able to send messages to millions of people with one click. Spreading across this new frontier is testing the speaker to respond to the need to change their style and content to appeal to much faster and multimedia-rich communication.

Therefore, the path towards public speaking is an endless evolution and creation. The tools and platforms are not the same anymore, but the essence of it all is standing strong: to connect, to inform, and to inspire. Public speaking, in all its possible expressions, remains one of the important strands forming the fabric of human communication, which is always undergoing modifications to respond to a vibrant world.

FAMOUS ORATORS IN HISTORY

The might of verbal language has stood the test of time throughout history as a decisive substance in the building of societies, inspiring movements, and sparking revolution. Throughout the ages, numerous people used this power, and some of them can be considered as the figures of eloquence and persuasion whose words can be heard in the halls of history.

Such a character is the ancient Athenian legend Demosthenes. Demosthenes was born in 384 BC and survived a childhood full of misfortune, such as a speech impediment, to become one of the most famous speakers of his generation. His iron perseverance and his self-training turned him into a genius of peroration. His oratorical works, especially the "Philippics," were inspirational pleas to exercise resistance to the growing menace of Philip II of Macedon. The fact that Demosthenes voiced the fears and hopes of the rest of the people in Athens made him a source of hope and an icon of resistance against tyranny.

Hurry along to the Roman Republic and we come to Cicero, whose elocution powers were unrivalled in his day. Cicero was born in 106 BC; besides being a statesman, he was a statesman, statesman and lawyer. His speeches, including the Catilinarian orations, were critical in bringing to light the conspiracies that were aimed at destroying the stability in Rome and also quieting them down. The eloquence of Cicero was not only in his mastery of language but also in his incorporation of logic, emotion, and ethical appeal, all of which flowed together. The legacy he leaves behind stands as witness to the effectiveness of rhetoric in the cause of justice and rulership.

This is the era of the Renaissance, which produced another giant of oratory, Queen Elizabeth I of England. Her Tilbury speech in 1588, when the Spanish Armada was threatening, is a legendary address in terms of issuing the call to arms and in terms of sovereign authority. The words of Elizabeth inspired her armies, making them feel invincible and part of an invulnerable nation. Her speech was an embodiment of the particular strength of individual charisma, with the effect of communicative strategy, which supports her position as an invincible leader.

Jumping over the Atlantic and reaching the shores of the United States, we come to Abraham Lincoln, for whom his famous Gettysburg Address is one of the most remembered speeches of American history. Founded in the time of the Civil War in 1863, this concise but deep speech changed the meaning of the existence of the nation and its devotion to equality. The effectiveness of Lincoln in delivering weighty truth in an honest and clear language displayed the timelessness of honesty and ethical clarity in speech-making.

Winston Churchill became one of the world-famous personages of the 20th century, whose eloquence was a bastion against the wave of dreadful tyranny during World War II. The inspirational words of Churchill, like the speech that was given in the event of, we shall fight on the beaches rallied a desperate nation and gave hope during the most dire of moments. He was a master of rhetoric in a way portrayed by his use of imagery, his manipulation of repetition, and his unquenchable spirit to the extent of embodying the meaning of resilience and bravery.

The speeches of these orators, among others, are epitomes etched in history. The power of oratory is forever eminent because of its ability to reach audiences, present visions, and move people into action. Using these historical examples as an educational example, we look at the intricacies of modern-day public speaking. We are taught through these lessons that business is just as much focused on the art of persuasion as it was in centuries past. The examples that these orators left behind them are the guiding lanterns of those who want to move hearts and minds by the power of the word.

WHY ORATORY MATTERS TODAY

Living in a time when digital communication and fast exchange of information are more and more prevalent, one should not overlook the importance of oratorical art. What is spoken is much more than the transfer of data; it is a connection that goes beyond data transfer and is intensely personal and inescapably powerful. And not only words but also their manner of delivery, emotions, and relationships they create.

In the truest sense, oratory is a very old profession that has continued to prevail even in modern times, where the world moves really fast. It functions as a means of persuasion, education, and inspiration. When written correspondence is sterile and deprived of the meaningfulness of face-to-face communication, the spoken word can thus provide life to the ideas, making them memorable and potent.

This is because the power of oratory today is as valid as it has ever been, since this means of communication may be used to penetrate through the clutter of the contemporary communication media. With social media, email, and instant messaging, the communication environment has been developed to favor concise language rather than deeper language. But in oratory, one can express oneself elaborately and expound with complexity in such a manner as to occupy the mind of the audience and touch its heart. A done speech is able to win the speech, and the speaker can express sincerity and emotion that is not easily produced in text.

In addition, oratory is important in leadership and governing. A skilled speaker will more likely lead an audience into support, change, and have a sense of unity among them. Their rhetoric is able to mobilize social action and win support for their views, reaching a wide array of people with answers and guidance during the vagueness of the uncertainties. Being able to verbalize a vision eloquently and consistently is a very potent tool, and therefore, Oratory is an essential skill of a person in a position of authority.

Oratory in any learning environment makes learning more interesting by helping to relate to information and create an impression. With the help of oratory methods, a teacher or educator can make the lessons interesting and make boring information turn into a story that will inspire them to learn more and use their analytical abilities. Oral communication is also interactive, and this ensures that there is a dynamic exchange of ideas, where dialogue and further understanding take place in the communication process.

Oratory also enables people to stand out in competitive fields in the professional arena of life. Effective use of words that are presented well and convincingly may open the gates to possibilities and partnerships, be it in business, at interviews, or during presentations. It is not confined to the sphere of industry, which is why it is priceless when cultivating relations, gaining trust, and achieving success.

Oratory is also crucial in keeping the cultural and historical stories alive. Telling tales orally has formed a very high point in human civilization, as it has enabled the traditions and values of a generation to be transferred to the next generation. Oratory remains a way in which various voices can be heard in the modern world, and in this manner, the margins are given a chance to express themselves and tell their narratives on a wider platform.

After all, oratory is important in this day and age as it represents the human aspect of communication. It brings us back to our common humanity, which bodes well with empathy and understanding of various perspectives. In a time when technology seems to be taking a toll on how we relate to each other, the spontaneity and genuineness of voice at work restores in us the thrill and the sheer beauty in human contact.

CHAPTER 2

Building Confidence

OVERCOMING FEAR

On stage, when you are before people, there is the thump thump thump heart beating, rather like the force of a beat of a drum. The palms are sweaty, and the mind is racing when it smells the pictures of the examination and verdict. It is a normal thing- the stomach feeling of fear when you have to rise before people and speak.

This is fear of the unknown to most people, a primitive instinct that tells people what is feared. The mind, being ever a watchdog, resorts to fancies of potential mortification and gets thence a chain of physiological processes in motion. The throat closes, the throat breaks, and the stomach quivers. It is in this confusion that the remedy of change lies.

The realization of what the fog of fear is will be on the path to getting rid of it. Fear is never the antagonist; it is the reminder, the caution of the critical state at times, and the gravity of what is about to come out of the mouths. By naming it, one will be able to beat its power. The fear of talking may be referred to as glossophobia, but it is not something impossible to fix. Preparation and practice are something to be offered in their place instead.

Lemuel Archer has said that confidence is founded on preparation. The act of organizing a speech and coming up with a well-structured speech is a process that creates a sense of control, makes sense logically, and can reach the heart and mind. When one is highly familiar with the issue at hand, it becomes a set-up so that he or she is not concerned about his or her fear but rather the message and the audience. This control further advanced with speech practice, rehearsing, speaking, etc. There is familiarity that is comfy, and familiarity through repetition.

The next tool against fear is visualization. In their minds, they practice how to speak, imagining the successes and how the audience will react to it, and their minds become accustomed to the practices. This kind of pre-visualization is capable of transforming the fear of something into excitement, turning a potential enemy into a friend.

Most people seriously underrate fear in terms of using breath as a warrior to overcome it. Controlled breathing in and out eases the brain and the body, the heart, and enables one to comprehend. This kind of magic of easy mindfulness anchors the speaker and allows them a chance to stay put on the field of a tempest.

The last one is to engage with the audience. Fear reduces upon learning to shift the interests to other people rather than oneself. Members of the joint experience are the readers who are not the opponent. They will allow contact making by looking in the eye, smiling, and an open posture, and it will initiate a presumption of empathy and understanding.

The difference can be experienced when the speaker is expressing himself to the people. The fear that seemed overwhelming in the past has turned into motivation to be healthy and have romantic desires. Trust increases where it travels round, and news wherever it goes, with no other inquest thereabout. As to the fact,

The overpowering of nerves does not mean the overpowering of them in the science of a speaker, but the use being made of them. What it resulted in is the acknowledgement that fear, when implemented and understood, may be a powerful weapon. The awakening, whether in the lives of the speakers or representatives in day-to-day lives, is that every speaker, despite the experience they might have, has the potential to overcome the fear of speaking to their audience.

The path that leads to becoming a good orator is, thus, not fearless but one that the light of fearlessness guides to go, so that it can be utilized to catapult towards the power of development and bonding. This is when it is time to get to the stage and become capable of speaking clearly, firmly, and confidently.

THE ROLE OF SELF-BELIEF

It is the age of modern presentations and bluffing, where a person has to speak convincingly and eloquently, using something that cannot be seen, yet is very powerful, which is self-belief. It is the inner belief that can drive the speakers who can make audiences fall in love with the magic of words. The silent self-assurance is what makes individuals get into a platform, a board room, or in front of a camera.

Self-belief is not a mere attitude of mind alone, but it is acting on a potential and capability. It is presented in how a speaker carries himself or herself, how he or she shoots his or her voice, and in how honest he or she is in presenting his or her message. This inner assurance that is familiar to the audience and can be likened to the invisible piece of string connecting the speaker and each listener in building the power of trust and connection can be felt.

First, from being self-aware comes belief in oneself. Knowing what is missing and what one can do well is one of the methods through which a presenter can bring his/her specialties and leverage what may appear as weaknesses as differentiators. This self-knowledge is similar to the sculptor who sees the potential in a block of marble that has never been tapped, and gradually, the sculptor knocks the layers off each other until the sculptor gets a masterpiece. Tolerance to weak sides and focus on strong sides are the ultimate steps that enable the contemporary speaker to develop a proper feeling of self-confidence.

They are the other pillar to the construction of self-belief, and they are dubbed as preparation. When a speaker is well prepared, he or she walks in with the impression that he or she is demonizing what he or she is addressing. This is not just about memorizing things, it is learning about one audience, you know what to ask, and are willing to change at the last minute when everything is going wrong. This type of preparation provides an individual with a sense of control and composure, and self-confidence flourishes regardless of the hard situation that may occur.

In addition to this, a visual image is among the weapons of the speaker. Speakers can train their show with the assistance of their imagination, because through the standpoint of vivid visualization of the successful speech delivery, the speakers can train their acting. The brain exercise gives a form of positive certainty, which will grow into the perception that one can get and thus be a winner. The visualization can fill the gap between possibility and actuality, and the dream of successful communication appears to be adjacent and true.

More to the point, being confident in oneself is not associated with arrogance or overconfidence. It is a practical faith which is based on experience, preparation, and a practical knowledge of individual powers. This kind of balance is necessary in that it does not give the speaker an opportunity to be complacent and to have no points of contact with the audience. So long as a speaker possesses a true self-belief, allows criticism, and is willing to change and modify skills, improvement occurs continually.

In the greater aspects of public speaking, self-belief is the spark that turns fear to excitement, uncertainty to clarity, and hesitation to action. It can help a speaker to risk giving a vulnerable talk and exposing the real self to the audience. Such realness is so heartfelt, and it has a long-lasting connection that transcends the borders of one speech.

Self-belief can be said to be the pulse of effective public speaking. It is the silent power that enables the orators to be above the shadow of doubt, to talk with passion, and thereby to influence change. In the era of modern communication reflecting all the peculiarities and intricacies of these processes, self-belief turns out to be one of the key allies that can help the modern speaker to achieve the horizon of his or her potential.

BODY LANGUAGE MASTERY

In the hectic modern world of public speaking, words run like a ripple that has gone on and on and on, and then decides to leave the stream altogether. There is a language not spoken that says so much yet says nothing at all. This is the communication that is referred to as body language, and is conveyed in pictures that are not full of word mix. It is a symphony of gestures, expressions, and movements that form a very important part of the art of oratory.

Consider the prospect of being on a stage, the spotlight on, and those waiting expectantly for you. How you sit, how you hold yourself, becomes the overture to your verbal story. Hold your head high, your shoulders up, be confident, and be able to make the members of your audience trust your message.

The artful movements of your hands, clasped in gentle poignancy, or animatedly gesturing by way of explaining yourself, become a visual aid. Purposeful gestures help to stress the rhythm of your speech, make the important points come out, and lead your listeners to a particular point. A big movement is an indication of a big concept, and a small movement can bring the audience into a smaller moment. Every step that you take is conscious and slow, and it layers your speech with context.

The windows to your emotions are facial expressions, and they can attract attention and capture the individual. The skeptical listener can be disarmed by a warm smile and made to understand the seriousness of what you say by a furrowed brow. Eyes, which are usually referred to as the mirrors of the soul, play a crucial role in making a connection to your audience. When you have direct eye contact, it gives a feeling of trust and honesty to your audience and will make them feel heard.

The area that you take up on the stage is body language, as well as the gestures that you use. The walk around the stage when there is a clear intention can indicate the shifts in your speech and cluster the audience. A step forward will give importance to a very vital sentence as a stand, where you are stationary or still, can make your words sink in.

The rhythm of your breathing affects the perception of your presence as well. Regular, even breathing shows poise, and ragged breathing is a tip-off of perplexity. This inner rhythm becomes aligned with what you say, and it makes the delivery very harmonious, which will connect with your audience.

Another little element of your body language is your clothes. Your attire must go together with your message so as to increase credibility and enable people to believe what you are saying, as opposed to the distractions.

The art of body language is not a division of learning body language and how to move in certain ways, or probably how to take up a certain posture; Mastering body language is being genuine. This is because when your body language and words match, your statements become complete and convincing as well as realistic. It is the art of appearing in tune with oneself and people.

The more you practice this aspect, the more you will realize that your body is your voice and can be used as a tool that adds strength to the message you want to get across and captivate the audience with. When it comes to public speaking, where each little detail counts in making or breaking a speech, body language is that silent accomplice, in that it takes your oratory to a whole new level, a notch above the average, a standing impression even when the last word does not come out of your mouth.

DEVELOPING A CONFIDENT VOICE

Public speaking is a skill that incorporates both the sound of words and the sound of the voice, and the latter tends to be the medium through which confidence is expressed. Modern communication is so full of noise, a reassuring voice sounds like a beacon guiding the audience through the hurricane of too much information. One needs to be aware of the foundations in order to develop such a voice.

This is how the trip starts: the breathing starts with the breath, the engine that runs when nobody speaks. Deep breathing, which keeps one focused on maintaining steady breathing, not only enables the projection of the voice but also relaxes the nerves, allowing the speaker to have a grip on the setting. Strength and stamina can be developed by practicing diaphragmatic breathing, which is a practice where the stomach inflates instead of the chest. This approach helps to maintain a continuous air stream flow that does not cause the voice to break or strain.

Then, the pitch, the tone, and the colors of the palette of speech are discussed. Pitch variability helps to keep the listeners alert so that they will not be put into a state where they want to sleep because of monotony. One that goes ever up and down, that murmurs and shouts, that attracts and fascinates, is interesting and memorable. It is not all about variation, who cares, but about authenticity. The tone should be a clear indication of what is in the heart and mind of the speaker to be able to bring a closer relationship with the audience.

It is also necessary to be clear and articulate. All the words must be pronounced correctly so that the message is brought out clearly. Tongue twisters and teaching reading out loud can improve these and make mumbling into clear talking. In addition, when one strategically pauses framing, then the audience has time to digest what has been conveyed and the speaker has time to compose themselves, which brings rhythm to the discussion.

Volume does as well. It ought to be manipulated based on the room size and the message. A loud projection is authoritative, and a softer volume is a more intimate one, which can invite the listeners and make them feel the intimacy and trust. Regulation of the volume is also a way to show flexibility and awareness of a speaker about his or her surroundings.

There is also confidence in the preparation. The mastery of the content gives the speaker a platform where he or she can deliver with certainty. Practice cannot cause uncertainty to be converted into certainty because the fear of forgetting is enshrined to induce the freedom to bear in mind, as they actively involve the audience. Self-recording and feedback requests can also guide and identify the areas of improvement and result in constant progress.

Finally, the body language accompanies the talking voice, and it supports the message of the speaker. An assertive posture that is upright and straight, with a good head held high, exudes power, authority, and composure. Gestures need to be effective, with the main focus being on the highlighting of points, though not distracting from the verbal part. Such rapport is achieved through eye contact with the audience, and it makes the communication more personal and effective.

The voice also becomes a tool of confidence, which makes the speaker an interesting personality and not just a messenger of words. The process of forming a confident voice is not the overall distance to go, but rather a continuous form of definition and adjustment. By every chance, the voice is more polished in the details of human communication, one that always gains impact on the listeners.

CHAPTER 3

Crafting Your Message

IDENTIFYING YOUR CORE MESSAGE

The first, and most basic, thing to do with any public speaking project is to determine what you are trying to say. It is the reason you say what you say, the reason that makes your presentation have the heartbeat behind the words that you speak, the reason that makes you and your audience connected. In its absence, speeches will be just a bunch of words that do not have any intention and do not have a lasting impression.

Just picture yourself on the edge of a forest, and each of the trees is an idea, fact, or anecdote. In this thick forest, you still need first to determine which way you are going to cut through the brush- that is your central message. It is the moral that guides your mind and helps it see only one thing when speaking out in words to achieve your final objective.

The first step to finding this main thread should be thinking over what you want to say in your speech. Do you want to inform, persuade, entertain, or inspire? It is also very important that you understand your intention because it directly determines how you construct your message and the tone in which you will express it. Take your audience into consideration, too; they will affect how well you formulate your fundamental message, according to their interests, their level of knowledge, and what they expect to find delivered.

Then, get to the crux of the matter that you want to discuss. Distill the most important information, the points that speak to you, and your points of need and beliefs on a deeper level. All these major points are to be reduced to one or a couple of sentences that summarize your point. It is usually known as a thesis, and this statement becomes a ballast of your speech, which makes things clear and focused.

When you start to shape up your key message, make sure that it is plain but strong. These are opportunities to fall into the trap of including too much so as to water down the effect. Rather, it is better to be simple and detailed, and to leave a message in controls without any unnecessary additions. A solid core message is a skeleton key, a guiding light, which both the speaker and the audience follow, and makes sure that every single word is part of the story that is being told.

Thereafter, after formulating your core message, it becomes the basis on which you construct your speech. This idea should reverberate throughout all of your efforts, including the intro and conclusion, and reaffirm its importance and make it resonate much more. The fundamental message must be supported by stories, statistics, and examples, and form a cohesive and persuasive story.

As soon as you get your center message out, this will be the basis you use in crafting your speech. Every detail, including the introduction and the conclusion, has to resonate with this idea, emphasizing its importance and clarifying it further. The tales about bad people, figures, and cases must all be used to demonstrate and defend the message and create a coherent story.

Furthermore, a central message can touch people even after the speech has finished. It remains in the memory of the audience, making people think and even change. This timelessness is what makes a good speech great, and it has an impression on the listeners; they remember it.

In modern-day public speaking, defining your key message is not just a background procedure, so to speak, but an absolute factor that determines how successful your speech is going to be. It is the media that makes you know that your words are orderly and powerful, and makes simple speech a memorable one. Before you step on the stage, make your main idea the one that serves as the guiding light to make you and your audience reach a starting point of understanding and closeness.

STRUCTURING YOUR SPEECH

Writing a speech that should be convincing and especially insightful is a challenging process, both in terms of planning and organization. This subchapter literally dives into the art of organizing your thoughts, or even information so that not only does it capture the attention of its audience but it actually goes in the extra mile of ensuring that the information you have according to your audience you have presented the information to the audience in a manner that leaves no doubts as to what is being discussed to the audience.

A speech is based on what it is constructed with, and one can equate the speech to a building's entire structure. Various parts of the speech serve various purposes, and the linking of the whole creates a whole. The introduction makes you ready, gets your attention, and sets the tone of what will be expected. This is the place where your presence is constructed so as to bring one close to the audience by providing a hook or a question of interest to the audience. It is now that you need to combine the element of curiosity and invite the listeners to take a tour of discovery.

The second most important part of your speech after the introduction is the body of your speech, since the most important part of the message should be found there. This is where you are supposed to know how to be exhaustive and how to make one lead to the other. You can adopt a more structured format, such as the question-answer type or chronologically, after all, it would depend on what your subject matter is. The major points are expected to be detailed effectively and should be backed with some facts, examples, or anecdotes that one can closely relate to. There is also a significant transition between points as it acts as a segment bridge to help the listeners understand how to follow one topic to the other.

The conclusion is the end of the puzzle, where you conclude your speech in a very pleasant way. It is here you message the key messages and leave an impression. It would be ending on equally strong; it would pick up not only the tune of the beginning, but it has a chance of changing up to the theme or the question that began in the introduction, and it would give a closeness and completeness of some kind. It is also an opportunity to encourage action or stir up thinking in the crowd so that they can think about the insights being put across.

When you want to structure your speech, one key thing you must relate to is the equation between content and delivery. You need to think about the structure that contributes to the overall message in your speech so that there is a cumulative effect to each piece of the message. You can also be accompanied by visual illustrations like a slide or even other props so that you can be in a position to justify your argument and also have the listeners entertained. These must be, however, taken advisedly: these must remain only additions to those verses which you are presenting in a speech.

The other important speech structure is timing. They have to allocate an appropriate amount of time to each section, ensuring that the speech is not rushed so much and that the paper is read at an appropriate speed. One way to develop this balance is through practice. You do have a feel for the pacing, and then pace accordingly.

The final effect will be that the structure of your speech will represent the level of intelligence you possess for the viewer and the message that you are attempting to convey. It is an emotional blueprint that can be used in lots of contexts and topics; however, it is premised on the principles of clarity, consistency, and interactivity. Having acquired the art of putting your speech in the most effective form, it is possible that you would get one of the greatest machines ever invented, which would transmute ideas into well-made stories that could impress any listeners.

USING STORYTELLING TECHNIQUES

Storytelling as an art form has a strong presence in the context of public speaking, creating a fabric of connection and inspiration between an orator and a listener. Storytelling goes beyond presenting the facts and figures. It turns the information into a story that is infused with life, which is presented in an interesting way to listeners and impacts them profoundly.

The art of storytelling in a speech is initiated when one develops a captivating narrative. Just like in the format of an effective novel, this arc has a sequence of a beginning, middle, and end, and there is also a smooth transition between them. The speaker makes preparations at the beginning, introducing characters and establishing the mood. It is not only an introduction but an invitation, which attracts the audience to a world where they could recognize themselves in the story of the characters.

Conflict is the heart of any story, and tension makes the audience sit on the edge of their seats. In the context of speaking in front of an audience, such a conflict can be presented in the form of a problem or challenge to which the speaker or characters are able to respond. By explaining this dilemma in a way that is quite easy to understand, the speaker makes the audience make an emotional investment, something to root for. Change is found in the process of traveling through this conflict, where it changes on a literary level as well as in the minds of the audience.

The vivid description of a story and the sense of certain things are also very important. Through the words used, the speaker creates a vision, and the audience visualizes, hears, and senses what is happening around. Descriptive language acts as a vehicle that carries the listeners out of their seats and into the phenomenon of the story. This use of the senses helps users to get more connected to this message and, in this way, it is easier to recall.

The importance of dialogue can also be used to improve the telling of a story in a speech. Characters are alive through dialogue, and their voices resonate the diversity in life as represented by their perspectives and feelings that bring the story to life. The speaker employs dialogue as a means of revealing character traits, motivations, and relations, thereby introducing more multi-dimensionality to the narrative. This interaction factor breaks through the monologue boredom, and it gives a chance to the audience to be the actors of the story.

Pacing to build up suspense and keep interest is another important point. The speed is different; the speaker rushes and slows down so that the listeners can enjoy every bit of her emotions. The breaking of the critical aspects with pauses brings intriguing anticipation; the listener has enough time to meditate and imbibe what is being communicated.

In addition, there is a powerful end that unites the story lines, consequently leaving a very smart and loud message. This last act is where themes and learning in the story are summed up, and the viewer feels closure and enlightenment. By being capable of relating the story to the main message of the speech, the speaker makes sure that the story does not become mere amusing entertainment but rather a source of deeper insight.

The problem is that storytelling has become one of the key components of the modern scenario concerning the sphere of public speaking because such stories turn speeches into memorable moments. Through the use of narrative, speakers are thus able to attract the attention of their audience, captivate and motivate them, and give them something to resonate with long after the speech or the word has been delivered.

INCORPORATING PERSUASIVE ELEMENTS

The influence of persuasion in the art of speaking deserves high respect as a brush stroke of the master painter who turns the plain canvas into an associated masterpiece. To influence people and change their beliefs, attitudes, or behaviors is not only a natural gift but can be developed through the strategic use of persuasive components by using systematic learning and practice.

Understanding the audience is one of the most important steps in the process of becoming a speaker, and the main point is to find an appropriate way to reach the people you speak to. Understanding the psyche of the audience implies the realization of their values and beliefs, their feelings, and the formulation of messages that will appeal as much as possible to individuals in their intimate capacity. Such an association is the fertile soil to which the seeds of persuasion may be planted.

First is the speaker: The credibility of the speaker is, first of all. The building of trust in the audience and authority with the audience is not an optional goal but a building block. A show of knowledge, integrity, and honesty may also be realized. When a speaker conveys their ideas with a sense of authority and confidence, supported by knowledge and genuineness, they are given respect and attention, and then persuasive communication can take place.

The appeal to logic and reason is known as Logos, and it forms the core of strong persuasion. Here, it is the speaker who has to create a tapestry of facts, stats, and evidence that he or she chooses each strand very carefully and precisely so as to support the general narrative. However, logical thinking should be presented in a logically clear and consistent manner so that the audience can follow the argument very easily. Complex concepts can also be elucidated further through the use of analogies, similarities, and vivid examples, which are very convincing.

The convincing power is more than sometimes in pathos, the appeal to the heart. Any person capable of touching the hearts of his/her listeners has got a powerful, persuasive communicative tool. This can be through storytelling, which is a very ancient method that engages and delights listeners, pulling them into a collective experience. Using fine-tuned stories, full of pictures and feelings, a speaker may induce empathy, strife, or even a sense of righteous anger, matching the audience's feelings with those that a communicator wants to express.

Rhetoric also supports the effectiveness of a speech as long as, of course, it is strategically used. The repetition, parallel lines, and rhetorical questions are examples of devices that help to stress important points and establish a rhythm and flow that is most captivating and even convincing. Such figures of speech are very powerful elements when used wisely and can turn the otherwise boring speech into a unique and unforgettable one.

Moreover, the timing and delivery of persuasive elements are crucial. The speaker must be attuned to the audience's reactions, adjusting the tone, pace, and emphasis as needed. A well-timed pause can lend weight to a crucial point, while varying vocal dynamics can maintain engagement and underscore the emotional undercurrents of the message.

Incorporating persuasive elements into a speech is both an art and a science. It requires a delicate balance of logic, emotion, and credibility, each element harmonizing to create a compelling narrative. By mastering these techniques, speakers can not only inform and entertain but also inspire and transform, leaving a lasting impact on their audience.

CHAPTER 4

Understanding Your Audience

ANALYZING AUDIENCE DEMOGRAPHICS

Knowing your audience is one of the most solid foundations of a successful speech, and it can bring your presentation a lot of success. It is diving into the colorful mosaic of the people you will be standing in front of, asking them to listen to you and open themselves to the varying personalities of all the people who have come to your show with their varied backgrounds, experiences, and expectations. Through investigations of the demographics of the audience, the sounds that are put across can be addressed to appeal to the audience better and guarantee presence and understanding.

Demographics cover a wide range of characteristics that include: age, gender, education, cultural heritage, and socioeconomic status. These aspects become important in the development of the audience's thoughts and interests. An example is that a presentation directed to a group of high school peers will be very different from one that will target industry experts. By being aware of such differences, the speakers will have the opportunity to modify their language, examples, and the general strategy to appeal to the level of understanding and interest of the audience.

Among the initial demographic factors, age is usually one of the first things that people analyze. Younger generations could be more related to the active discussions with multimedia components and anecdotes. On the other hand, the older audience might find a more classic style that is more appealing, clear, and concise, and has information that is backed up with credible data. Speakers may be able to achieve sustained interest by matching the age to the style and content of the presentation to create a sense of relevance.

The other demographic element that can be used to sway the audience is gender, though a more subtle factor. Gender knowledge assists in choosing appropriate language and subjects that do not isolate or discriminate. It is inclusive and respectful, and creates an environment of comfort among all listeners. Similarly, the influence of a population is shaped by its cultural background, thus creating a certain reaction in the audience. The message can overcome cultural boundaries as long as the differences are recognized and respected to overcome the divide and eliminate an exclusive environment.

Another very important element is educational background. In communicating with the audience, where educational backgrounds are different, one should find a compromise between complexity and clarity. Too technical language can lose the audience, and oversimplification can lose the audience that has a high level of knowledge. When speakers can accommodate the level of their listeners, or those who are listening, then it can be easier to determine the nature of the education level, so that what is being brought out is something that everyone will understand.

An audience is also impacted in its reception of a message by the socioeconomic status, but the effect thereof is less perceptible. It may influence the examples or situations that are regarded as closer to those people, and their attitude to some problems. These differences should not be overlooked, as being aware of them will enable speakers to select more relatable references and analogies that will not make any assumptions that might discourage the audience.

At the end of it all, the study of the audience demographics is all about establishing a connection. It is all about targeting the audience, the kind of people you are communicating with, and their way of thinking, so that it is not just heard but felt. This knowledge creates a conversation, not a monologue, which imparts involvement and gives an atmosphere of exchange of ideas openly and freely. The way to have more impact by means of a presentation is by customizing the presentation to the distinct of the audience to ensure that the reception not only goes in but endures past its boundaries to register well outside of the entire presentation.

ENGAGING DIVERSE AUDIENCES

The listeners are not all the same lump in the vast landscape of contemporary oratory and exchange of ideas by way of entertainment and stories. Rather, it is a fabric embroidered with similarities and differences of experience and point of view. Every thread is a different story, a different voice that makes part of a bigger buzz of an audience. Being aware of this diversity is very important to any speaker who wants to connect past the surface to the depths of every listener.

The initial action in reaching such a heterogeneous audience is to identify the range of heterogeneity there. This diversity includes cultural background, age, gender, socio-economic and educational background, and even individual beliefs. All these factors may affect the perception and reception of a communication. Consequently, a speaker should be able to think about being inclusive and flexible in his/her approach to the audience.

A dynamic and empathetic style needs to be used by a fluent speaker in order to approach different listeners carefully. This also entails the development of messages, which are universally acceptable but contextually done to recognize the peculiarities of the populace. Available language is one such method where unnecessary jargon or colloquial language that would turn off or be ambiguous is avoided. They want to create a bridge of communication where all the listeners would be part of the conversation.

Storytelling is an effective mechanism in this effort. The narratives are above cultural and personal boundaries and provide a shared territory on which different audiences can make contact with the speaker and with one another. A speaker can find the common experience that unites all of us by telling moving stories with a lot of emotion. This not only catches the attention of the audience but also creates a sense of community and belonging to a purpose.

Nonetheless, cultural sensitivity and awareness studies, in a way, trigger the challenge of communicating to various audiences as well. One needs to keep cultural nuance in mind, and one should not stereotype or make a generalization that may offend unwittingly. Such sensitivity ought to also be applied to the recognition of alternative styles and preferences of communication. An example is where certain cultures may attach importance to being direct and assertive, and others would want to be more indirect and subtle. Adjusting to such differences can play a major role in making the communication process very effective.

Additionally, it is possible to add interactive features that would work wonders. The experience can be more inclusive and democratic with the inclusion of audience participation by being allowed to ask questions, conduct discussions, or conduct active polls. This not only legitimizes the existence and views of the audience but also sets the mood, making it even more positive with respect to active listening and interaction.

Multimedia and visual aids may also be necessary to reach out to different people. Well-developed visual images can cut across cultural and language communication to provide the third level of cognition. Nevertheless, it is vital that these supports have to be culturally relevant and available to every member of the audience.

Essentially, the most striking factor in reaching various audiences is that the speaker should be in a position to listen more than speak. When a speaker truly gets to appreciate that a room full of diverse individuals is real, he or she can make messages resonate not just in the room, but in a far-reaching way that reverberates long after one leaves the room without the speaking event. By doing so, the idea of public speaking is no longer the mechanism through which information can be disseminated but rather a lively exchange of ideas that is able to praise and appreciate the rich variety of the human experience.

ADAPTING TO AUDIENCE FEEDBACK

Depending on the audience's reaction, things can change and become very fluid in the world of public speaking; having the ability to adapt to audience reactions is not just a skill; it is a form of art. We as presenters are poised on the edge of perception with raised eyebrows, nodding of the head, and murmuring of the lips, weaving the speech of silence between us and our audience. Be aware of such little messages, and correcting yourself accordingly can make a good speech turn into a resounding and memorable one.

Reading a room with open books and every page is an expression, every posture, and every thought being entirely unspoken is like observing the audience. No audience is alike, and their review may differ as much as the difference in their background. Speakers need to develop their observational powers and be sensitive to how hot or cold a room is. Your speaker must be sensitive to such cues because once you are aware of them, you can skillfully manipulate the cadence of a speech, and you can leave your speech heard as well as felt.

Active listening is one of the most effective tools when it comes to this process. This is not only listening to words, but knowing what emotional things and considerations might be involved. Speakers need to seek answers by talking to audience members before and during the presentation so that they are in a position to compile these answers in their presentation. Either through direct engagement or by monitoring the response of the listeners, listening skills will help speakers make adjustments to their delivery so that listeners can understand more.

Take into account the fluctuations of involvement in the audience. There can be cases when a start speaker will see a plea of interested faces with which he reads every word. When this is the case, exploring more sophisticated concepts will be helpful, and the conversation will be richer. On the other hand, when the audience looks distracted, the performance seems to be losing their interest; they may need to adjust in terms of tone, pacing, and content to gain their attention again. This flexibility enables the listeners to be part and parcel of the discussion as opposed to being viewed as subjects of information.

The feedback may also be expressed more specifically, e.g., in the form of questions or comments to a Q&A session. Such interactions are a rich source of generating views of audiences and issues. Responding to such queries intelligently and with a sincere interest can help the speaker establish a rapport that itself contributes to the effectiveness of the speaker. Composing and delivering answers decisively and clearly, thus becoming quite more credible, is a skill that not only strengthens the credibility of the speaker but also shows respect toward the views of the audience.

In addition, non-verbal communication is also an important part of the feedback loop. Eye contact, gestures, and posture of both the speaker and the audience continue to flow communication. Maintaining eye contact also allows the speaker to have an interpersonal connection that is beyond words, and more often than not, an atmosphere of trust and openness ensues. In the meantime, attention to the body language may provide hints about the degree to which a given audience member is engaged in the presentation and may serve to guide adjustments to the presentation styles or tone of voice used.

Finally, the adaptation of audience response is a dynamic process. It should never be seen as a one-time thing, meaning there is both intuition and empathy with the audience that needs to be factored into the process. Entering this maze of a dance, speakers will learn how to be more receptive and effective speakers who can make an impression. Airing on the sides of audience responses, speakers can not only improve their respective performances but also positively impact the experience of their readers with the help of a common exploration and perception.

BUILDING AUDIENCE RAPPORT

Creating a bond with an audience goes beyond the use of words; it is the delicate art of creating a cloth of trust, knowledge, and emotions. This is a very fundamental part of public speaking, and it does not simply entail the sharing of information but building a common ground that makes the speech and the listeners meet in a two-way traffic. The main idea behind the development of rapport is to connect with the audience and appeal to their emotions, values, and expectations.

The first second's count. An open body language, along with a warm, confident smile, sets the mood. Eye contact, posture, and gesture used by the speaker must portray openness and accessibility and must make the audience feel like the speaker is part of the same experience. It serves as a non-verbal communication, and this kind of communication counts more than words, creating something unspoken, thus making receptivity better.

The first thing to consider is the reader. This will necessitate a keen sensitivity to their demographics, interests, and cultural backgrounds. By adapting the speech to the expectations and experiences of the audience, it is possible to create the notion of relevance and respect. The audience will also be mobilized to contribute when they feel understood; this will turn passive audience members into active members.

Anecdotes and stories can also be a brilliant tool. The speaker is humanized through stories, and this makes them approachable and accessible. With personal anecdotes, where such is in order, comes a chance to reduce the distance between the world of the speaker and that of the audience because there exists a commonality of the story that rises above the individual differences. These stories not only capture the audience but also play the role of carriers of the feelings and values that the orator should express.

A good tactic is also humor, which is applied sparsely. It is capable of breaking borders magically and creating a camaraderie effect. The element of laughter is a common denominator that unites every individual because the speaker is perceived to be more popular and genuine. However, comedy must be culturally sensitive and considerate of the audience.

Another important part is active listening. Although it is always viewed that public speaking is one-directional communication, it is, in an actual sense, a two-way communication. Embodiment of the audience reaction, evoking the tone accuracy, pace requirement, or content by their signal, and recognizing their response and input can improve the amount of rapport. This is a viable technique that expresses the value of the participation of the audience, strengthening the bond.

Another important role is played by language. The connection could be reinforced by selecting vocabulary that appeals to the listeners in terms of their experiences and feelings. The diverse language that accommodates the heterogeneity of the audience is also inclusive, which encourages a feeling of belongingness. In addition to this, clear and simple communication puts the message within reach of everyone as it eliminates the barriers posed by misunderstanding.

After all, rapport is all about sincerity. People watch and are easily able to judge ingenuity. Raw enthusiasm and the sincerity of a speaker are something that is catching, making one trust and adore them. The speaker who is being genuine to themselves and their subject matter has automatically pulled the audience into their frame of reference and by doing so established a mood of mutual respect and understanding.

The skill of establishing rapport with audiences is not a skill, but an art in the land of current public speaking. To leave a mark, it follows the balanced jointness of verbal speech and non-verbal signing, understanding, and sincerity. This bond formed between the speaker and the audience changes the process of speech into a mutual experience that benefits both the audience and the speaker.

CHAPTER 5

The Power of Words

CHOOSING THE RIGHT WORDS

When it comes to such an art as talking in front of masses, the choice of words is a key that opens the doors of interest and comprehension among the people. The words do not only carry the information, they are a lively messenger of emotions, intentions, and shades. The art of correctly selecting words is a fine art in the correct mixture of definitiveness and imagination, accuracy and drive.

The place where effective communication starts is the ability to model language to the audience. It is important to know the demographic and psychographic profile of listeners. Do they operate in the industry, or are they new people? Are they young students or aged professionals? The words and the tone should appeal to the level of knowledge and interest of the audience. The lecturer's address to an audience of technical experts can go into a lot of detail, jargon, and complex terminology. In contrast, the same information would be simplified and put in context for a lay audience.

Word rhythm and flow are also very important in the delivery of public speeches. Like a composer who composes a symphony with notes, a speaker should use words to form sentences that will sound like a symphony. The flow of speech may impress a crowd and make them engage in the story, which makes them listen to that particular speech. Silences, as well as words, mean everything, giving time to think and accentuate.

Imagery and metaphor are a part of public speaking that help to make abstract subjects turn into living pictures in the minds. A well-chosen metaphor can help bring a point into focus, make it stick, and be relatable. As an example, terms that will make a strong visualization are used to describe a complicated change in an organization and to provide a metaphor for sailing through turbulent waters. With their appropriate use, such linguistic devices can contribute to an improved understanding and retention.

Persuasive communication can benefit in many cases by the simplicity of its foundations. Plain language, which is not complicated, makes the message understandable to everyone. But simplicity is not to be confused with dullness. An excellent orator employs the high end of the language by incorporating elegance in the sentence structure in a very powerful way.

Words have too much emotional load. The right words can prove to be inspirational, motivational, and can evoke someone to take action. They are able to induce laughter, crying, or a feeling of belonging. The words used by a speaker should be deliberate as they influence the tone in which he or she wants the discussion to seem. A compelling story that can develop an emotional attachment to the audience is one where the narrator shares some anecdotes and personal stories.

Accuracy in the use of words is the key. Vagueness or ambiguity may result in a lack of understanding or a lack of interest. All the words must serve a purpose, which is the larger message. This demands careful planning and insight into the matter. A presenter has to be good at self-editing his/her words and determining and rejecting repetitions and fillers.

Along with the verbal language, there are all these non-verbal elements of speech, gestures, facial expression, and intonation. The aspects go hand in hand to communicate and uphold a message. Body language helps to bring a complete communication experience where a speaker punctuates what is being said with their body movements to make it more dynamic.

After all, the very art of selection of the appropriate words is a balancing act that is propelled by knowledge, empathy, and creativity. A speaker needs to be a great observer of human nature, tell stories, and have mastery of language. The selection of every word used can make a speaker make a simple speech and make it unforgettable and life-changing to the listeners.

THE IMPACT OF TONE AND INFLECTION

The inflection and the tone of what you say can be as powerful as the words in a place like public speaking, where every word is thoroughly thought out, and every pause is a choice. The intonations of a speaker make a simple sentence turn into an interesting story, which brings out emotions and makes the listener imagine. Tone and inflection do not serve the purpose of just being decorative items but rather the lifeblood of effective communication, as they create brilliant pictures in the minds of the listeners and fill the gap between the speaker and the audience.

Think of the pitch of a voice that swells and breaks like the swell and the fall of the waves of the sea. The effect of this back and forth can be relaxing, stimulating, and demanding, and the result is that listeners are pulled so deeply into the speaker's universe. The modulation of a voice can be used to emanate a sense of authority, empathy, or urgency. The raising of the voice by a notch is what can make a question into a command or a statement into an invitation to a conversation. Tone and inflection are the secret spices used to give words their strength.

Think of a speaker who has to tackle a room that is full of anticipation. Their voice sounds very alluring, and they welcome and begin their work; the tonality is that of being welcome, and there are friends. They have some inflections in the important moments, sounding the key moments of the idea and underlining the importance of what they are saying. The audience listens intently, not only to what is said during the speech but also to how it is said. That is the science of oratory, where a monologue is turned into a dialogue, an exchange of a few well-chosen words that will echo in the minds of the audience long after the words are heard.

The influence of tone and inflection is felt especially when it comes to the impression of sincerity and credibility. The use of a confident tone will create a sense of trust, and a wavering, unsure tone will plant a sense of doubt. Inflection also contributes to the formation of the perception. When the sentence ends in a rising tone, it may be used to bring up uncertainty, whereas a falling tone gives assurance. They are rather soft but effective tools of persuasion that can turn over the opinion of the audience and make an impression.

In addition, tone and inflection also play a role in expressing emotion. A friendly tone can be soothing, and an angry one can be passionate. Such vocal components convey the speaker's feelings to the audience and establish a sensual bond with them. This connection to the emotions is what makes a public speech a deeply human activity, to the extent that exchanging information is only one part of the picture.

Living in a world where email, text messages, instant messenger, and other forms of digital communication seem to remove the layers between people, the tone and inflection in any speaking is even more important than it used to be. These details give words their reality, and make them multi-layered and evoke a feeling of expressiveness and urgency. They are the strands that knit the fabric of a speech, and make it a story, a story that inspires and motivates and moves.

To become a master of public speaking is to invoke the strength of sound and inflection and understand that these elements will convey a message, invite emotion, and it will form a bond. It is to learn that it is not so much what one says as how one says it, and the voice is a potent tool that can create a marvelous ability to deliver a spoken word. Tone and inflection in the hands of a polished speaker have become instruments of transformation, and speeches assume the high form of symphonies of thought and sound.

CREATING MEMORABLE PHRASES

A catchphrase is like a tapestry in a speech where one is able to create a catch phrase, which draws the audience back into the speech, into their minds permanently. To compose such phrases is an art, and it is not the wording that matters, but the rhythm and the tone of these words and their emotional content. A good phrase can be used to render a speech interesting to a stunning level, and a good phrase acts as a lifesaver that helps one through the speech.

First of all, it has to be simple. An example of a memorable phrase is one that people can quickly comprehend, but with a depth of meaning. That takes a fine choice of words that are precise, descriptive, and even. It is usually simple; a sentence being overly complex might end up losing meaning. Take into consideration the strength of repetition, which is capable of inculcating a message into the minds of the listener. Other than supporting the message, repetition has an effect of inventing a rhythmic cadence that may contribute to the recall.

One is the use of imagery, which makes it important to have phrases that remain in the mind. Reaching into senses, the speaker will be able to describe vividly using words in order to create concrete elements out of abstract things. In that matter, metaphors and similes are a powerful means; their use enables the formation of the parallels between something that is already known and something unknown, thus making complex concepts more accessible and interesting. An example is introducing a difficult situation as a "stormy sea," which can give rise to an emotional feeling in the audience and encourage them to hold onto the idea.

There is the soundness of the words as well as what they mean. A musical tone can be added to the phrase by the usage of alliteration, assonance, and consonance, so that it becomes easier to listen to and memorize. The way in which the phrase is rhythmic, staccato, or flowing can contribute to the emotional reaction of the audience. An acute, snappy wording may signify severity or emergency, whereas a pleasant music-like wording can bring a feeling of peace or reflection.

Emotional appeal is what drives a catchy phrase. An appeal that appeals to the heart has the power of whipping up an audience to her thoughts or actions. The phrase can create this emotional connection in terms of storytelling, where it will become a focal point of it. When a speaker identifies the values, beliefs, or desired aspirations shared by the audience, an alignment of the phrase generates a bond that is stronger than that of the mere circulation of information.

Lastly, context gives a background in which a witty statement may glitter. When one knows the reader as well as when and why a speaker is speaking, it could help him or her narrow down his or her language so the phrase given makes sense and is also effective. A phrase that works well in one situation loses some effectiveness in another, and that is why the concept of adaptation is so important. Being in touch with the specifics of the time enables a speaker to utter a phrase that is not only amazing but memorable as well.

The capability to come up with memorable lines is an indicator of the dexterity and expertise of the speaker in terms of spoken communication. It is an adaptation of art that involves and mixes linguistic accuracy and emotional and human intelligence, which would make a very powerful tool that could convey inspiration, persuade, and unite. Speech characterized by such art ultimately allows the speaker to take his/her communication to new heights and have an indelible impression on the audience.

AVOIDING COMMON PITFALLS

The act of public speaking is an art that involves a finer form of balance between preparation, confidence, and versatility. Experienced speakers can also fall into many of the same traps that destroy their effectiveness and influence. Becoming aware of such possible pitfalls and avoiding them can rescue the performance and credibility of a speaker to a greater extent.

Along with many other traps, one of them is the excessive use of notes or slides. It is easy to understand how such tools can be helpful in structuring the presentation and making sure the most important ideas are discussed, but relying on them too heavily may also take the interest out of the speaker addressing the audience. It is very necessary to have a balance between visual aids and eye contact. The person presenting in front of the audience by simply reading off notes exposes themselves to possible loss of attention by the audience, in addition to looking unattached to the subject matter.

The other common pitfall is not preparing enough. It is well-known that confidence is normally based on good preparation and being familiar with the material. A speaker cannot overlook the value of rehearsal; any speaker who misses this may end up struggling to get the words to communicate, as the listener may not obtain an organized communication. This may result in the loss of self-confidence that the audience can easily notice. Mock presentations with friends, working in front of a mirror, or even recording can also offer good feedback and confidence.

When a speaker ignores the audience, it is a big mistake and can turn away the listeners. Succeeding in public speaking depends on the capacity to reach the audience, which involves listening and watching. The knowledge of the interests and backgrounds of the audience and the expectations will enable the speaker to adapt the presentation to meet the expectations. When a performer cannot adjust to an audience, every kind of feedback, whether it is non-verbal or verbal, the crowd may become bored and lose interest.

The other risk is boredom or monotony, which can easily dissolve the potential of a presentation. Such a speaker who takes one tone or speed in his/her speech runs the risk of boring the listeners. A difference in the way of delivering the voice, e.g., changes in pitch, speed, and loudness, is able to keep the audience interested and place stress on essential aspects. Also, the use of pauses allows audiences to learn and to have the next details in mind.

The audience can become overwhelmed, and the essential thing can be lost in too much information. Speakers can think that they have to prove their knowledge by telling too many details in their speech. This may, however, confuse and prevent the audience from memorizing important information. The message must be boiled down to its most important elements and made visible and to the point.

Failure to control anxiety is one of the common problems that may ruin a presentation. Being nervous is a normal thing, yet a lack of thematic control over the anxiety may result in a range of different ways, including trembling fingers, stuttering speech, and an empty head. It is important to come up with solutions to control anxiety through taking deep breaths, visualizing, or grounding exercises, in order to remain calm and focused.

Finally, the inability to end the speech properly may make the audience have no idea about what the speech was about and/or what the takeaways were. At that, concluding remarks must reaffirm the key points and offer a catchy closing phrase that would echo in the mind of the audience. It is a chance to impress and give the chance to reflect or act further.

These are some of the pitfalls that speakers should avoid, and by avoiding them, they are able to improve their public speaking skills. They are able to deliver presentations that are engaging, impactful, and memorable. Awareness and lifelong learning are the best way to prepare a successful public speaker, as one can make every presentation a moment of learning and connecting with people.

CHAPTER 6

Visual Aids and Technology

EFFECTIVE USE OF SLIDES

Visual aids are the tools that cannot be ignored in the field of contemporary public speaking, as they greatly contribute to delivering information and memorizing it. Slides are undoubtedly one of the most effective forms of presenting sophisticated thoughts quickly. Strategically used, they can make a dry presentation a lively story that makes people listen to it.

Slides act as an illustration of what the speaker is saying, or is trying to get across to the audience, a roadmap to what is being discussed. Articulated well, they are informative and they help to drive home points, thus enabling the audience to have an understanding of the topic at hand. Slide design must be very clean and purposeful, as you do not want to confuse and overwhelm your audience with excessive clutter. The simple design that utilizes generous white space allows the reader to focus on the key facts and to absorb them as well.

The selection of the color scheme is an important factor in the power of slides. The colors are to be selected in a way that fits the theme of the presentation and maintains the same appearance throughout the rest of the presentation. The significant difference in the readability between text and background makes it accessible to the audience, as their eyes do not need to be strained to keep up in reading. Moreover, sensational use of colors may not only make a person feel some emotions but also emphasize necessary places where the attention of readers and viewers should be.

Typography is the other essential aspect that ought to be chosen carefully. The fonts are to be readable and have professional fonts, which should also vary in size to show hierarchy and significance. The decision to pay attention to the font across the presentation makes the design look cohesive, and the intentional use of authors could be used to highlight essential parts by bolding or italicizing them.

Graphs, charts, and images are the three visual aids that are more effective in conveying data and concepts than language alone. They are to enhance the word of mouth and not to substitute it. Appropriate graphics can convert abstract concepts into reality, and complex information known only to the experts can become understandable to the audience. It is, however, vital that such visuals are of good quality and also sized so that they are not pixelated or distorted.

Transitions have a dynamic effect on fruits and animations used sparingly in presentations. They are capable of keeping the audience interested and highlighting the change of subjects. Nevertheless, the overuse of shiny animations may take away some of the messages and should be avoided. The idea is to supplement rather than to compete with the narrative of the speaker.

Another factor that is important in the use of slides is timing. The slides should be presented in length that is long but not so long that the flow of the presentation will be altered. The presenter should arrange his or her pace in accordance with the slides so that there will be a smooth flow of the content.

In the end, the goal of the slides must not overshadow what the person says. Emphasis must be made on the speaker and not the slides, which should serve as a background aid that makes understanding and memorization more successful. With the help of design and delivery of slides, the speaker can master his work and make his presentation memorable to his audience. A well-placed use of slides makes most talks more than just discussions; they can be remembered as sessions aided by the visual and the spoken, using the slides to give a good story.

INCORPORATING VIDEOS AND IMAGES

The current fast-paced environment of present-day public speaking has seen the introduction of multimedia aspects, including videos and images, into presentations, making them dynamic and interactive. Visual elements are used to draw the attention of different audiences. As a speaker attempts to keep audiences engaged, the ability to use visual elements is an essential skill.

Videos and images can be useful in improving the message delivery as they offer a visual description of the story that was added to the verbal words. They can explain complicated concepts, touch people emotionally, and bring them closer to the audience when used properly. As an example, a beautifully placed video clip may bring out an aspect better than a long-winded explanation, and pictures may bring out emotions that may not be able to be brought out by words only.

The use of video in a presentation enables speakers to cross the limit of purely spoken presentations. Videos may add a moving quality to introduce diversity to the viewers and distract them from a monotonous speech. A brief, powerful video may be used as a strong introduction, giving the whole presentation a tone, or as a strong ending, which will produce a strong impression. In addition, testimonials, product features, and presentation of statistical data in graphically appealing ways can also be presented with the help of videos.

Instead, images can be used as an effective way to reiterate the important points. One picture is worth a thousand words, and gives one an image that could be used in memory recall. The speakers will be able to make the audience feel that they are part of the story by introducing images that the target audience relates to, with a better sense of the story. Images, be it a moving photo, a de facto chart, or a funny cartoon, will enrich a presentation with a new sense of profundity and dimension.

Nonetheless, the use of videos and images cannot be done haphazardly. All these elements must be appropriate to the subject and add something to the general message. Too many or poor-quality visuals can subtract credibility from the speaker and lose the attention of the audience. Thus, it is essential to choose high-quality images that go along with the theme of the presentation.

Technicalities are also crucial when multimedia is integrated smoothly. The speakers are also to make sure the equipment they will be using is provided and in excellent condition. Those videos and images are operating with the presentation program. By being acquainted with the technical arrangement, any inconveniences have a chance to be avoided so that the speaker is focused on getting their point across.

Besides the technical competence, speakers are advised to be considerate when timing and pacing multimedia is incorporated into the speech. Images and videos should be incorporated into the presentation in a way that there are no breaks in the speech, like between videos. Silence at the right moment will enable the viewer to internalize what he sees, and simple indications may steer them through the story.

After all, using videos and other pictures in conjunction with verbal speech is a matter of finding the right balance between visual and text media in public speaking. When handled intelligently, these features can turn a presentation into a memorable event that would make an indelible impression on the participants. Taking the power of multimedia, a speaker will be able to take his or her presentations up a notch, thus ensuring that his or her message will be felt long after he/she has spoken the last word.

USING TECHNOLOGY TO ENGAGE

Technology has become a part of our lives in our modern, fast-developing society to such an extent that it has enabled us to communicate, work, and interact with one another differently. The changes have not spared public speaking, which is an ancient art. It is not the method of using the newest gadgets or software; it is the ability to use them to improve communication and interaction with the audience.

The scenario here is that you are in a stage with the light pointing on you, but rather than stage an ordinary monologue to your audience, you can actually give them a powerful experience of interaction. Technology enables the speakers to go beyond the borders, and presentations become more engaging and interesting. Slideshows, videos, and animations are good visual aids that can be easily incorporated into speeches so that they can facilitate visual stimulation along with verbal communication. Such tools assist in expressing complicated concepts, visual representation of information in a digestible manner, and the engagement of the audience by changing the sensory stimulus.

In addition, technology also enables real-time interaction with audiences. Applications such as live polling tools and question-and-answer sessions help the speakers connect with the audience. Through reaction questions or rapid-fire polls, presenters will be able to know the understanding of the viewers, preferences, and responses almost immediately. This helps not only to make the audience feel part of what is going on but also to help the speaker modify their delivery to such an extent that they are close to home on the general feedback they receive.

Public speaking has gone even further with the usage of social media platforms. It has the potential of events being streamed in real time to people around the world, across geographical boundaries, with the chance of a greater spread of ideas. The use of hashtags and the writing of social media posts also allows a hum of the event, in which people will be encouraged to actively participate in and discuss the event with both others attending and people watching at home. Through such systems, speakers get to communicate with their audiences before, during, and after their presentations, and this forms a community and uninterrupted interaction.

Virtual reality (VR) and augmented reality (AR) are pushing the limits of what is possible in the field of public speaking. These are immersive technologies, providing the audience an opportunity to connect with content on a whole new level. Consider a presentation on climate change in which people feel as though they are literally taking a walk through a forest, or they are viewing the melting ice caps. This may result in an emotional appeal; translate abstract notions into reality, and the consequences of such an experience will remain in a lasting impression on the audience.

Nevertheless, the incorporation of technology in oratory does not come without its problems. It involves a delicate balance so that what is being transmitted is not by means of technology but in spite of technology. There is always a possibility of facing technical problems that can interrupt a presentation, and speakers should have fallback plans. Also, excessive dependency on technology may make us forget about personal connection, which is another key aspect of the effective character of the speeches delivered.

In conclusion, effective application of technology in public speaking can be best based on the prudent use of technology. It must be an extension of the voice of the speaker, which helps tell the story and support the message. Technology, when applied wisely, can turn a traditional speech into a dynamic and interactive learning process and can attract the attention and imagination of the audience in a whole new manner that remains inconceivable so far. Taking them on board, the speakers will be able to reach their audiences on a new level, and thus, their words will feel better than just being heard.

AVOIDING TECHNICAL GLITCHES

The use of unified technology has become fundamental in the world of modern-day speech. However, despite all the advantages of technologies, unexpected difficulties caused by them might occur and affect even a properly organized presentation. The issue boils down not just to the mastering of content but also to the skillful use of technological resources that one will have.

It is most important to know what you are making use of. Being conversant with the gadgets, be it microphones, projectors, laptops, or clickers, would mean that you know how to fix very simple problems that could befall the gadgets in a jiffy. It is always recommended to be at the place of work early enough to carry out a proper check-up of the equipment. Here, it is carried out by ensuring all devices are charged up, coupled up, and working as expected. It can be avoided by testing microphones in terms of clarity and volume, checking projector alignment, and ensuring that all of the multimedia will work with the presentation software.

It is always good to expect problems and be prepared to avert them so that a speaker may be relieved of such undue tension. It is a good idea to have backups at hand. An example of this would be where the presentation is dependent on a PowerPoint or other program, and having both a printed version of the slides and an alternative form of media (digitally stored) in the form of a USB has proven to be of great assistance in such circumstances. Moreover, it is good to do research on the Wi-Fi capability in the venue and always to have an offline version rather than online-based materials to avoid connectivity problems.

Rehearsals must not be disrupted. Such rehearsals enable the speaker to practice in a real presentation environment, within which it is easy to detect and sort out the various possible technical snags. It is also important to rehearse in these sessions with the transition of slides and multimedia at ease and with a professional touch.

Having a group of technical people can be very reassuring. Building a relationship with the technical staff in the venue enables one to tap their knowledge. In case of opportunity, it is better to have a specified team member of your own company so as to get things straight, plus control and knowledge about the technical issues is greater.

Despite the most careful planning, sometimes things go wrong in terms of technology. The mastery of a speaker lies in the way he or she copes with these difficulties and does it in a composed and graceful manner. Having a positive demeanor when there is a technical failure calms the audience and convinces them of the integrity of the presentation. It is useful to have such a back-of-the-mind checklist of troubleshooting steps to apply just in case some glitch occurs. Being able to think on one's feet and be able to proceed with the presentation, having no back-up to technology, is an art that is learned over time.

It is crucial to communicate with the audience in case of technical problems. Citing openness regarding the circumstances (a hint of humor included), it is possible to turn what could have been the most awkward silence into a bonding experience with the audience. The time can be spent usefully by involving the audience in a short chat/question and answer session, which can help pass the time until certain matters are sorted out.

The modern world of public speaking cannot be imagined without adopting technology. Nevertheless, the trick is to find the right balance between its advantages and the possible trappings and make sure that technology is used as an asset but not an obstacle to the message. Preparation, rehearsal, and the ability to be flexible are all aids that can help speakers deal with the complexity of presentations in modern times and present that message clearly and with confidence, no matter what technical issues arise.

CHAPTER 7

Handling Q&A Sessions

PREPARING FOR QUESTIONS

The only start to a speech event is when one steps on the stage. In addition to the prepared speech, a speaker should be willing to expect questions that can be asked after the presentation. The skill of answering questions calmly and with authority may greatly influence the impression. In this subchapter, question preparation is tackled as one of the most important skills for a modern-day speaker.

Forecasting questions is one of the most important steps in learning about the audience. A presenter is supposed to study demographics, interests, and possible concerns of the audience regarding the issue. This will enable the speaker to guess what kind of questions may come up. As an example, a technically oriented fan base can start asking questions related to the newest technology. In contrast, a cascade of environmentally aware people can concentrate on the issues related to sustainability.

The other key element of preparing questions is developing an effective speech. A well-organized presentation that explores the subject in detail does not give much opportunity to be confused and misunderstood. At the same time, it is also necessary to admit that any speech, no matter how profound it is, cannot exhaust all the overtones of the subject matter. Therefore, skills training in answering questions means ensuring that we know possible holes or areas in response that can be addressed in a query.

In addition, practicing possible questions is a productive practice. It is brainstorming questions that may be asked in accordance with the speech content, as well as the analysis of the audience. There is no better practice than calling on the aid of colleagues or friends to pretend a Q&A session. The exercise will not only assist in the development of articulate answers but will also help one to develop confidence in response to unforeseen questions.

Other than rehearsing, a speaker should also come up with a plan for handling the Q&A session. These encompass defining limits at the start of the session, including time to ask questions and preferred format to bring up such queries. In this way, such measures keep the session systematic and on track.

Listening is yet another essential skill in the Q&A session. It is always necessary to listen carefully to the question that is posed in order to give an answer that is relevant and makes sense. When a speaker is asked a question, he or she is expected to maintain eye contact with the one asking the question, and in case of a need to paraphrase the question before responding, he or she can wait a few moments to formulate the thoughts in his or her mind. Not only does such a strategy show respect to the audience, but it also gives the speaker the chance to give a more thoughtful response.

There are other situations when a speaker will face difficult or even unimaginative questions. One is required to be composed and calm even when some tricky questions are raised. When someone asks a question beyond the knowledge of the speaker, there is nothing wrong with admitting that and promising to come back later. Credibility can be created by bringing honesty and transparent information that creates trust on the side of the audience.

Lastly, one indispensable component that helps in sharpening the skill of dealing with questions is feedback. Following the presentation, it is advisable to get feedback from close peers or mentors to act as an eye-opener on ways to do it better. It can also be said that the queries administered and answers to them can enrich their ability to do so in a future setting.

This is to say that, as important as a speech itself, preparing to respond to questions is equally important. The ability to handle it can quickly turn a speech into an interactive discussion, impress the listeners, and make the speaker a credible and confident communicator. Questioning as an art is no longer confined to answering the questions, as it is an art that helps to connect with the audience and enrich the effect of the presentation as a whole.

ADDRESSING DIFFICULT QUESTIONS

When it comes to performing before an audience, that instant when someone asks a question seems like an epiphany of light in the most remote points of a theatre. There is the art of making answers that no one really wants to know, but through them, the course of the presentation may ride and ultimately the presentation package. The current chapter explores the subtle tactics of managing such questions gracefully and without losing control of the situation.

Questions are sometimes the connection between the thoughts of an orator and the knowledge of the audience, as an orator stands before the audience. Special, though, difficult questions can challenge this affiliation, which makes the speaker think on his/her feet and be in control at the same time. Listening is the initial condition to answering such questions. Active listening not only shows respect to the person asking the question but also enables the person asking the question to make the speaker fully understand what they are seeking to ask.

After comprehending the question, it is very important to take time to mull it over. This little bit of thought gives the speaker the time to think of a logical answer. In some cases, silence may be off-putting, yet it is an effective strategy that may exude consideration and self-assurance. It is during this pause that the speaker can organize his/her thoughts in his/her mind and therefore, render a well-formulated and apt response.

When formulating a response, one should be as clear as possible. The simple and to-the-point response can not only render the questioner satisfied but also strengthen the position of a speaker on the topic. One must stay calm and collected even when the question is offensive or when it is controversial. To appear confident, it is also possible to keep the same tone and proper body language so that any tension can be diffused.

Also, show respect in recognizing the views of the person asking the question, even when they are the opposite of what you believe. Such a recognition does not mean consent, but knowing their opinion. On verifying the concern of the questioner, through such a procedure, the speaker may develop a more mutually supportive environment, which opens the pathway to making an effective discussion.

Another useful tip is to think of the hard questions one might need to answer before giving a presentation. Responding to questions more confidently, the speaker may address the Q&A session more easily by listening to another perspective and assuming possible answers beforehand. This foresight enables one to discuss the questions, even unforeseen ones, appropriately.

When faced with a question that cannot be answered immediately, honesty is the best policy. Admitting that further information is needed demonstrates integrity and a commitment to providing accurate answers. Offering to follow up with the questionnaire after the presentation can help maintain credibility and demonstrate a genuine interest in the audience's concerns.

Finally, redirecting the question to the audience can be an effective strategy. By inviting others to share their insights or experiences, the speaker can transform a challenging moment into an opportunity for collective learning. This approach not only alleviates pressure from the speaker but also enriches the discussion with diverse perspectives.

Being able to tackle challenging questions changes potential pitfalls to your advantage by giving you an opportunity to connect and develop. It says a lot about the flexibility of the speaker and his/her capacity to connect with an audience. By listening attentively, speaking wisely, and with an open mind, the speaker can also get through these situations with grace, making a lasting impression of being confident and competent.

KEEPING CONTROL OF THE SESSION

The most important skill in this constantly changing environment of public speaking is to have control of the session. It is not only a matter of getting oneself heard or how to perfectly give a speech, but it is also the way of finding how to reach the unpredictable side of human communication, to make sure that the goals of the session are achieved with efficiency.

The first few minutes of the speech are the most important. And when the speaker goes on to the scene, there is anticipation. This is where the most important thing is to create a sense of authority and relax. A confident posture, a pause (intended to get attention), and easy eye contact across the audience may establish the tone for the rest of the session. The orator has to exude the image of readiness and confidence, so that the audience can be sure that everything is under control.

After one has started a session, it is necessary to have the audience actively participating. This does not actually mean talking down to them, but it means developing an interactive environment. Rhetorical questions, anecdotes, and even pauses of a certain strategic nature encourage the audience to engage their minds and emotions. In such a way, by doing it, the speaker currently not only keeps it under control but creates a connection that can carry the interest and attention of all the participants throughout the session.

But it does not mean hardness. An effective speaker has to be flexible, as he or she has to be able to react to whatever is happening in the room. This implies having a sense of what the audience is doing, whether it is a slight movement in the posture or a whisper of agreement or approval. By taking these clues, the speaker can change how he or she delivers it, possibly explaining a point that strikes a chord or quickly skipping through something that lacks interest.

Controlling such situations also entails dealing with interruptions effectively and gracefully. Whether it is an off-guard question, a malfunction, or an interruption, the speaker is required to overcome the problems without the stream of thought being impaired. Taking the interruption in stride by being calm and amused, especially kills tension, and the session is likely to progress well. The speaker can be unfazed, which is a sign of security to the listener and maintains the session on focus.

The very format of the session can be extremely important in controlling. The presentation should also not be very confusing, and having clear transitions and a logical flow of presentation helps. Marking essential points and highlighting the main outcomes during the session might reinforce learning and help the audience keep in line with the message provided by the speaker.

Another important factor of control is time management. The use of the scheduled time is a sign of respect for the time of the audience, and it will also help the speaker gain credibility. Practicing the presentation with the time limit is useful because it is possible to feel the flow of the speech, which requires natural pauses and communication. This type of preparation prepares the speaker to be able to raise and lower the speed of the session.

After all, managing the session is all about exercising authority with the ability to appear friendly, structure with flexibility, and engagement with calmness. It is an art and cannot be learned but must be practiced, thought out, and come with a good sense of being aware. Through this art, a speaker is not only able to convey what he or she wants but is also able to leave a certain mark or trademark on his or her audience, making the session not only effective but also memorable.

ENCOURAGING AUDIENCE PARTICIPATION

Public speaking as an art has turned out to be a lively exchange of views between the audience and the speaker. In the context of recent presentations, connecting with the audience has become one of the most essential factors in presentational success. The speaker is the most important person in the scene with the light, but the audience is imperative in establishing the narrative. The natural symbiosis of the speaker and the audience is capable of making the monologue a dialogue with a sharing of ideas, where there is a symbiosis of community and purpose.

Setting up the environment where people can easily interact starts with involving the audience. Understanding the backgrounds, interests, and needs of the attendees is important to accommodate the message in a manner that they will appreciate. This relationship provides the basis of interaction since participants are bound to interact more when they feel that they are heard and understood.

It is very important to create a hospitable atmosphere. The body language of the speaker, tone, and openness are the main factors that have a great effect on the audience in deciding whether to participate or not. Welcome, open body language, and a big smile will allow a shared venture. These non-verbal feedbacks indicate to the audience that they are welcome to contribute to the audience and thus talk out their minds and questions.

It is possible to make the presentation interactive and include elements, so the audience maintains interest and participates in the presentation. Living polling, questions and answers, group discussion, etc., are techniques that encourage people to exchange ideas and views. Such interactive spots not only make the one-sided lecture-like presentation more interesting but also give these people control over what they create together.

The questions that are strategically asked may be another effective method to interest the audience. Rhetorical questions are able to elicit abstract thought, whereas direct questions are able to elicit unsustained responses. The speakers may have fruitful conversations by asking questions that pertain to the audience's experiences or concerns and deepening the subsequently formed discussion.

Technology comes with new means of increasing audience participation. Speakers are also able to induce real-time engagement via virtual polls, quizzes, and feedback tools via the use of the apps and digital platforms. The technologies enable participants to contribute anonymously, which will facilitate contributions from individuals who are reluctant to make announcements face-to-face.

The use of audiences should also allow the audience to be heard when they contribute in a good manner. Before reading, it is also important to close comments or questions and represent understanding of the input by the audience, and that collaboration is regarded. By incorporating audience response during the presentation, the speakers may be able to adjust their message to be more relevant to the audience and its needs and expectations.

Further, narrative is also a good way to engage and attract the audience. The ability to connect with the audience can be done through narratives that stir emotions or are akin to mutual experiences. As long as people present in a story think they can see themselves in the story being narrated, they will tend to be a part of the story and contribute their own experiences and thoughts.

After all, the theme is to promote the involvement of the audience so as to change the one-sided flow of the delivery of the talk into a two-way process of communication that facilitates the sharing of ideas. When the audience is satisfied with the talk, they are engaged, and thus they become contributors to the discussion, making the presentation deeper and more effective. It appears that the capacity to achieve exchange of good relationships with the listeners or viewers is one of the main aspects of successful public speaking, even as it is still developing. Accepting the principles of participation, speakers will be able to provide the chance to remember and be impressed by the whole process.

CHAPTER 8

Dealing with Stage Fright

UNDERSTANDING STAGE FRIGHT

A mixture of feelings arises when a person anticipates performing on a stage. The heart may start pounding, the palms can get clammy, and one may suddenly feel an otherwise unexplainable shiver running down their back. This is sometimes known as stage fright and is a complex fabric with the fiber consisting of self-awareness, vulnerability, and the natural human instinct of a desire to be seen in a positive light when in the presence of other people.

Stage fright boils down to the strong fear of being judged. When one is talking to people, he/she feel intensely that there are too many different eyes and cars staring and listening to them. This increased feeling of self-consciousness can escalate our insecurities and lead to the mind spinning about thoughts of being an inadequate person. There is an intimidation about every word and motion to be analyzed, criticized, and judged to the point where it is blinding, making it appear to be a mental wall that one cannot surpass.

Physiologically, stage fright causes a chain reaction of responses similar to those found in situations of real hazards. The body takes the fight or flight response when it feels threatened. Adrenaline spreads in the bloodstream to gear the person up to face or flee what he/she perceives as danger. It leads to a chain of physical reactions: the heart starts beating faster, breathing becomes shallow, and one can notice a tightness in the muscles. The response is instinctive and part of human evolution, but may be distressing when the mind has no clue about an actual threat.

Stage fright is also a complex emotional experience. It is not just a fear but a confrontation of barriers of anxiety, excitement, and anticipation. In other people, the fear of speaking in front of others is often mixed up with perfectionism. Spontaneity and naturalness may be squashed by the pressure to put up a perfect show, resulting in a stiff and rehearsed piece that does not connect meaningfully to the audience at all. Some will also have a contrary feeling of fear and excitement because there may be an irresistible appeal of the idea of exchanging ideas and connecting with others.

It is an important step to understanding the causes of stage fright in an effort to counter its impact. Understanding that it happens to all people, no matter whether they are new speakers or professionals, can give relief and make them feel connected. Also, the willingness to accept physiological reactions not as threatening, but as natural, can assist in reframing the experience so that the person can use the empowering feeling of energy to their advantage.

There are a lot of practical measures aimed at overcoming stage fright, and this is an individual approach. Controlled breathing, visualisation, positive affirmations, etc, are some of the techniques to help quieten the mind and the body. Deliberate rehearsals and practice can enhance self-confidence and even change fear into concentrated and active energy on the stage.

Stage fright is frightening, but not something one cannot overcome. It proves the strength of the human mind and body, reminding us how much we grow and how strong we can be. Realizing its essence and adopting approaches to cope with it, people can change stage fright into an advantage that promotes forceful and fascinating oratory. The process of conquering stage fright does not entail overcoming the fear part. Still, it does entail getting to know oneself more and one's audience more, and as a result, communicating more effectively and more profoundly with others.

TECHNIQUES FOR CALMING NERVES

There is the possibility of being in front of a large or small crowd of people, and that can give a feeling that may lead to a whirlpool of feelings, and the major one is a scattering of nerves, which may be too much asked of you, as well as unwanted. The knowledge of how these nerves can be quieted is essential in making a good speech. This subchapter dwells on the methods that may aid in turning the anxiety into a method to maximize performance.

Deep breathing is one of the best techniques for calming down. The method is to inhale slowly and with as much room as possible through the nose so that the diaphragm is able to rise as high as possible, and then to breathe out through the mouth. Such a small, everyday activity not only helps in the oxygen balance of the brain, but also in awakening the relaxation response of the body, lowering the amount of stress hormone. Before going to the stage, deep breathing can be performed to attain a feeling of power and composure.

Another strength that comes to the bag of tools of a public speaker is the visualization. Speakers can rehearse positive and successful ways of giving the speech to get ready for the day itself. The perception of the event to include only an amicable and encouraging audience changes the perception of the event to a manageable one. Such a change of attitude can diminish the anxiety level greatly.

Another technique that may also be utilized to relieve tension is called progressive muscle relaxation. It is achieved by tensing the muscles and gradually relaxing them, starting at the feet and working up towards the head. This practice not only aids in establishing areas of stress, but it also aids in relieving it so that the speaker may feel freer and at ease.

In addition, one should not underrate the effectiveness of positive affirmations. Such inspirational mantras as I am ready and " I am confident or I am looking forward to presenting my ideas will change the inner dialogue of a person, bringing self-doubt to self-confidence. These affirmations are also very helpful when one says them frequently and instills a feeling of confidence deep in the psyche of the speaker.

Another strategy that can be used to lower the level of anxiety considerably is physical exercise. The activities, such as jogging, yoga, or even a simple walk, will assist in releasing the endorphins, which are natural mood boosters in your body. Physical activity is a benefit because it enhances mood and aids in the process of burning off excess adrenaline, which is often a result of being nervous.

It is also very important to shift perspective and not think of self but about the message. When the focus is set on the value of the described information instead of individual performance, the speaker will have a chance to move the focus away from the thoughts causing anxiety. This audience-focused thinking not only eases nerves but also makes the presentation of the talk better.

Lastly, rehearsing the speech several times can make one feel familiar and comfortable. Speakers can give impromptu rehearsals through a mirror or even a few people giving constructive feedback to the speaker so that he/she can perfect his/her delivery. Being less anxious is most likely to occur when a person is more familiar with the contents.

These techniques should be included for everyone, which can turn the overwhelming experience of speaking in front of people into a way of connection and sharing. Speakers can achieve this by calming down their nerves, and the result is energy to deliver a point that is well felt by the audience, where anxiety is taken as a friend as opposed to an enemy.

PRACTICING RELAXATION TECHNIQUES

In the busy life of speech and public speaking today, everything frequently depends on going out with a sense of calm and confidence, which makes the difference between a good speaker and a great speaker. Speech art has much more to do with it than the simple expression of words; it is the control over the inner position. This control starts with the use of relaxation methods, which are an important tool, and they help the speakers to come across confidently.

Just think of facing a crowd, the lights on your face are blazing, and all the faces in the place are upturned in anticipation. This is a situation that may cause a chain reaction of physiological reactions in many, such as a racing heart, trembling hands, and a dry mouth. These will be the normal responses of the body towards the stress of public speaking. Nevertheless, by consistently following relaxation procedures, speakers will manage to convert this nervousness into energy and enthusiasm.

Controlled breathing is one of the pillars. This method refers to breathing deep and slow breaths that involve the use of the diaphragm as opposed to the chest. This allows a speaker to regulate his or her breathing by concentrating on deep, deliberate breathing so that the heartbeat can slow down, the nerves are relaxed, and thoughts can be gathered together. This seems the simplest of exercises, yet its benefits are far-reaching as the voice becomes settled, the mind becomes clear, and one grows able to concentrate and be clear in mind.

The other extremely useful technique is progressive muscle relaxation. These are the systematic processes of tensing and relaxing various body muscles. The speaker first of all learns to recognize tension and release it, starting with the toes and going up to the neck and the face. The practice not only relieves physical strain but also develops an increased sense of the body and helps one to root and feel stable.

One of the powerful weapons in the speaker's arsenal is visualization. The method involves speaking the speech silently and calmly in a relaxing place. Telling oneself in detail about how the process is going to unfold, that is, by visualizing the step-by-step process of walking on a stage and hearing the applause, a speaker will be able to develop confidence and calm down. Seeing how good it is to pretend that you are there and talk to someone makes you get familiar with speaking situations, allowing you to turn whatever fear you had into expected success.

Mindfulness meditation is a very important practice that can develop the capacity of a speaker to be more present and attentive. Investing in mindfulness, a speaker also obtains the ability to disregard distracting thoughts and admit them. It fosters a high level of consciousness of the moment so that the speaker can relate better with their audience and also convey their message on a very real level.

Relaxation techniques are not one-time hits, but they are ongoing processes that need improvement. By introducing habits into their daily lives, speakers develop a store of tranquility that may be reached in moments of demand. This devotion to self-domination changes the public speech process, which is a challenge to the chance to improve both self-awareness and meaning.

Considerations have to be given to the skill to control his or her internal world in the environment of contemporary public speaking, as important as the speech itself. With the incorporation of the relaxation strategies, the speakers can give themselves the means to go through the challenges that the speaking experience presents with élan and poise. Communication is a process that cannot be discussed only in terms of what one says, but also in the way in which he/she says it. It is through the practice of relaxation that one can make the most perfect communication.

BUILDING STAGE PRESENCE

Stage presence is an abstract element that makes a speech more than a simple presentation of the notes. It is the power to capture the interest of an audience, to put across an impression of confidence, and to appeal to the emotions of listeners. Building this presence is equivalent to creating a good performance, where a gesture, a pause, and an inflection build into the fabric of involvement.

Stage presence is all about self-awareness. It is very important to know their strengths and weaknesses, whether it is the pitch of a voice or the body language. Such self-perception gives an orator an opportunity to employ the inherent ability and improve on those aspects that need polishing. Confidence is something that is commonly mistaken to be inherent, but it can be developed with practice and preparation. The more a speaker is conversant with his/her material, the more confident the speaker is when delivering his/her content, hence bringing out his/her personality.

Physicality is a crucial determinant in constructing the stage presence. It is the non-vocal communicator that accompanies the oral words. The open body, maintained eye contact, and thought through activities express confidence and encourage the audience to become involved. Every action must be significant and not distracting by having unwarranted gestures that may not add much to the message. It is a balance between movement and stillness that is the secret, and each should be utilized so as to twist points made, or to keep it interesting.

Stage presence is supplemented by voice modulation. A voice is a really flexible tool that may express emotions, underline certain things, and help to keep the interest of the audience. A deep, slow, and loud delivery can be changed to a more penetrative performance by the change of modulation, speed, and accent. It creates a rhythm when the audience can digest information and guess the forthcoming surprise when using it.

To develop stage presence, it is important to connect with the audience. It is not about talking to them but also about listening to them and adjusting according to their response—body language and observation of facial expressions give a hint on whether the message is present. Being flexible and able to respond to the feedback of the audience at the moment of delivery shows flexibility and creates a touch of closeness and urgency.

The setting also brings about stage presence. Answering the needs of the environment and turning to the positive advantage is what can add a better overall value to a speech. The speaker has to recognize some acoustics and spatial dynamics, whether they are in a small room or a large auditorium. Active movement during performances on the stage, use of space in order to achieve stress, and being able to make the audience feel like they belong to the performance are all crucial elements.

Effective stage presence is based on preparation. This does not just mean being familiar with the material, but also practicing the presentation. Recording oneself in front of the mirror, recording something, or getting feedback from peers could also give a good hint about what could be done better. Presence is made up of confidence, and familiarity gives confidence.

Stage presence is also, finally, on truth. What attracts people to speakers is genuineness, sincerity, and passion in speaking. This is the genuineness combined with the delivery technique, which creates the impression. They can make themselves feel comfortable by reaching self-awareness, putting self-awareness into the use of body language, voice modulation, interaction with the crowd, and preparation, so that they could walk on the stage with having control over the crowd, which would make them go well with their speech, edging the process of the category of an artform.

CHAPTER 9

Practice and Rehearsal

IMPORTANCE OF REHEARSAL

When it comes to making a point and having poise and eloquence to characterize the effectiveness of a speech, rehearsal becomes the key to effective communication in the world of speech-making. Rehearsal is more of a dynamic exercise that is not limited to a memorization exercise; thus, it is used to perfect delivery and build confidence as well as perfect the effortless sharing of ideas. This is why rehearsing is like any performer, whether it may be the musician who is becoming perfect in his concerto, the artist in his craft, or the sportsman in his performance.

One such thing that rehearsal grants to a speaker is familiarity and comfort with his or her speech to move through the complexity of it with ease. It gives them the chance to internalise what they have been reading so that instead of being words on paper, they become a living story with a natural flow. This change is paramount because it allows the speaker to go beyond the ramifications of a script and be genuine in his/her endeavors with the listeners. By practicing it over and over again, speakers learn the rhythm and flow of the speech, so that they can add emphasis to the significant ideas and vary tones to keep the audience interested.

More so, rehearsal is an effective instrument for discovering and correcting possible pitfalls in a speech. It gives a chance to practice the ways of expression, gesture, and tone to find out what sounds best. The repetition ensures that a speaker can have a better grasp of the content to an extent where he/she would be able to answer questions even during the speech. Through practicing in a mirror or recording the training sessions, speakers can learn much about his/her body language and how he/she swings his/her voice, thus making the necessary adjustments to help and create clarity and impact.

Self-confidence that is achieved by practicing a lot cannot be underestimated. It forms the foundation of successful speech-making. Being well-prepared takes away most of the anxiety and helps one feel confident enough about not missing a single line or losing track in the middle of the speech. This exudes outward and creates credibility and trust in the eyes of listeners. An experienced speaker gives out a calm, confident attitude, and this enables the audience to hear and enjoy the message being delivered.

Also, the rehearsal provides the formation of the individual style and voice of a speaker. Practice can help the speakers to experiment with different techniques and approaches and identify what suits their personality better and is relevant to the audience. This is a priceless introspection by this very speaker as it enables them to establish a truthful connection with their audiences, evoking a sense of sincerity and relatability.

The fact is that pre-training must not be understood as a simple warming up; rehearsal is an important part of the process of speaking to the masses. It changes the abstract to the real, the theoretical to the practical, and the normal to the extraordinary. Through the process of rehearsing, speakers gain the instruments necessary to present their presentation in a way that will be compelling, impactful, and memorable. The thread of preparation, confidence, and authenticity flows through the tapestry of rehearsal, and when completed, creates a story through the tapestry of public speaking that captures and inspires.

EFFECTIVE PRACTICE TECHNIQUES

Practice as an art in the field of public speaking is a science and an art. So, to be proficient in this skill, somebody has to train through conscious and systematic practices that develop the nuances associated with delivering a speech. Repetition is the basis of effective practice, but surpasses rote learning. Speakers need to live in a world where they can mimic real-life scenarios where they are supposed to speak and get used to different situations and people.

One of the pinnacles of practice is comprehending the principles of voice modulation and articulation. Presenters must use emotion in their voices by varying the pitch, tone, and volume. This venturing also helps in creating an adaptable vocal range, such that what the speaker says is addressed to different people. Pausing strategically can and should improve any speech in its effectiveness. The audience will have time to digest and cogitate on the information provided.

In addition, good practice involves body language. Speakers need to keep in mind their posture, gestures, and facial expressions since these are also very important non-verbal messages that will shape the perception of the audience. The best advice on these factors is to practice in a mirror or recording to get a good idea of what you can learn, then speakers can feel free to practice their stance and how to portray a body language that supports what is being said.

Another crucial aspect in the development of the art of public speaking is feedback. Peers, a mentor, or a coach can engage in constructive criticism where helpful suggestions can be offered in areas that the speaker feels they need to improve. Group practice in the form of workshops can also be a supportive process in terms of group feedback, along with watching other speakers. The participatory style of teaching helps promote growth in the subject, in addition to understanding effective ways of communication.

It is an effective practice to simulate real-life conditions. The speakers ought to practice in situations that simulate those of their real-life speeches. This would involve practice in different environments, e.g., a huge auditorium or small conference rooms, and application of any available equipment, e.g., a microphone or a projector. Such trainings make the speakers familiar with different acoustics, lighting, and spaces, which makes the speaker less anxious and increases confidence when the actual presentation occurs.

Also, a very important part of practice is time management. The speaker must be aware of the time available to deliver the speech and then practice giving the speech within the time limit. That is in terms of prioritization, succinctness, and clarity. Scheduling can also be practiced with the help of a timeframe through which the speaker can understand the pace associated with the presentation and adjust accordingly to ensure that the audience continues to be interested.

A visualization serves as an effective practice method in the arsenal. Prior to presenting the speech, the speakers can visualize the speaking scenario by formulating answers to questions such as what it feels like to answer questions, subconsciously anticipating the reaction of the audience when it comes to their performance. This imagery is able to build confidence and also lessen performance anxiety because speakers will now be accustomed to the experience, which focuses on where they will stand on the stage.

Lastly, it is essential to develop a culture that is continually improving. Practice: Effective practice does not take place once in a lifetime, but it is a lifelong experience. Speakers can always improve and evolve in the process by taking up the opportunities to become better and welcoming new techniques and approaches to dynamic public speaking. This commitment to practice also makes them good communicators because they know how to engage their audiences and motivate them.

SIMULATING REAL-LIFE SCENARIOS

Living within real-life situations is a very good practice that cannot be taken lightly when one wants to perfect his/her public speaking. Such an interactive style of discussing the topic will enable the speakers to be ready to deal with many issues successfully and collectively. The creations of the surroundings that resemble any possible speaking experience help to understand the complexity of delivering a powerful speech.

The establishment of a realistic setting is one of the key areas when it comes to the simulation of real life. This is done by having the location where the speech will be presented, the nature of the people listening, and what the event is. Replicating each of these factors allows a speaker to get used to the environment they are to face and thus alleviates stress, which results in better delivery. This can be seen in an example such as practicing in a room with similar acoustics, and the floor layout of the venue will allow one to get an idea of how voice projection and movement may have to change.

Another important aspect of the audience simulation is that knowing who the audience is, what their interests are, and how they might respond to what is being said enables the speakers to address their messages better. Introducing a practice with a group of peers capable of role-playing as the audience will give appropriate feedback and assist in predicting questions or objections. This interactive element makes a speaker super-sharp when it comes to restrictions to interaction with many different audiences and attention on the fly issues.

It is also a good idea to insert some unanticipated challenges into these simulations. Live speaking situations tend to include the problems that could not have been foreseen, including technical issues or hecklers. These aspects, when incorporated in practice sessions, enable speakers to come up with tactics that will help them regain composure and adjust their talks easily. As an example, in order to be less distracted and communicate easily when the microphone goes wrong or there is some bothersome noise, it is possible to train the speaker to stay focused and talk easily under pressure.

Further, timing plays a critical role in simulating real-life situations. Speech practice should follow time limits so that the speakers get to learn how to allocate their time effectively, so that they can fit in all their important ideas within the time limit. It is a field that introduces the element of time, which is extremely important to ensure the involvement of the audience and make the speech as efficient as possible.

A part of this preparatory activity is to provide feedback. Positive criticism by peers or seniors is worthwhile in getting information on what needs to be changed. Increasing a feedback culture also enables orators to perfect their speech, improve their pace, and even their general projection. The constant improvement and final polished performance come with repeating, according to the analyzed repeated iterations of practice, with every iteration comes new feedback that is focused on in the next session.

Lastly, it is essential to have an emotional element during the simulation of the lines in public speaking. Communication is not all about words; it is all about communicating feelings and building connections with the listeners by reaching into the person. Speaking about situations that would bring real emotions to the speaker, one can train using this technique to put life into the text and to make one's speech sound human and appealing to the listener.

To sum it all up, the art of creating real-life situations in the area of speech performance is a complex task. It demands careful attention to the details and the readiness to accept the peculiarities of real-life circumstances. The practice through immersion allows speakers to develop the abilities required to bring memorable, riveting, and impressive presentations in any context.

FEEDBACK AND SELF-ASSESSMENT

Self-assessment and feedback in the sphere of modern public speaking are just as important as speech. The above factors are like the compass that takes speakers to clarity, effectiveness, and engagement. An outside observer (a member of an audience, a mentor, or the self-evaluative process itself) provides feedback that is reflective of the subtleties of delivery, message clarity, and general effectiveness.

Receiving feedback is an art that should start with an open mind. Those who give a speech should receive feedback in the mind that it is a method of development rather than an evaluation of the character. Positive comments provide information about the perception of the audience and point out both goal areas and areas to improve on. A piece of feedback given well may provide light on some of the elements of a presentation that might be unclear to the speaker, including non-verbal communication, tone of voice, or the frequency of discussion.

During the integration of feedback, the process must have an orderly framework. Feedback is something that speakers should actively solicit and that should be found in a variety of sources so that the speaker will have a clear idea of how he or she is doing. This may be considered by getting the feedback of peers and mentors or by employing digital facilities where it is possible to encourage the anonymous audience's response. Various views of different people can bring out various aspects of the presentation experience, which would bring a complete picture of the experience.

Self-assessment is the self-measure of their responses. It is a profound inspection of one's performance, with additional scrutiny of every aspect of the presentation's delivery. It is a process that allows the speaker to single out the strengths and weaknesses within themselves and thus embarks on a perpetual process of self-growth. The self-assessment activity may be organized in many different ways, including video recording of the speech, self-questionnaires, or reflective journals.

Self-assessment starts with the establishment of definite and quantifiable results. Such objectives are review criteria that the speaker can use to assess his or her performance. In comparing the real performance with these goals, the speakers will be able to know that there are discrepancies, and by doing this, they can zero in on areas that they need to work on. Also, self-assessment will motivate speakers to share their success with others and strengthen their positive behavior and confidence.

Although these two roles have differences, they are inevitably linked to one another. They create a dynamic cycle in which feedback guides self-assessment, and self-assessment refines the capability of accepting and accommodating feedback interpretations. This synergy initiates a culture of being better people because speakers are motivated to perfect their skills and ensure great presentations.

The contemporary orator has to maneuver through a world that is surrounded by a variety of audiences, and they all have their expectations and likes. Feedback and self-assessment in this regard become inevitable tools. They enable speakers to adjust their style, content, and delivery so that they can address the audience to whom they have to communicate, so that their message can resonate in the mind of the audience members and prompt them to remember it.

With persistent efforts to utilize feedback and methods of self-assessment, speakers can change their skills in public speaking so that every presentation is an action that works on continuous improvement and connection. This repetition process is not only to fix the mistakes but to have practice, to be able to work on their craft, to master the art of communication, and finally to become an effective and sure orator. When speakers incorporate this feedback-self-evaluation loop into practice, they begin an endless self-improvement path without ever ceasing to strive for new heights in the world of speechmaking.

CHAPTER 10

The Role of Humor

INCORPORATING HUMOR EFFECTIVELY

Humor is another mighty tool in the world of a public speaker, the thing that could turn an ordinary presentation into something totally unforgettable. It is a strategic use of humor that not only brings the audience but also builds a bond between the speaker and the listeners. It serves as a medium to destroy and melt boundaries and foster a comfortable, talking climate.

Knowing your audience is the key to integrating the use of humor in your speech. A sharp edge in understanding the demographic, the cultural background, and the overall mood of the audience is a must. Humor is relative, and what one finds funny to one group might not be funny to the other as well. That is why it is important to adjust your humor aspects so that they are understandable to the general audience. It is possible to know the humor level of the audience by examining their behavior when they are negotiating with them.

When to insert humor into the speech is also another key issue when it comes to humor in public speaking. A thoughtful joke or funny anecdote will be able to bring a charge to the room, with badly timed humor having the potential to break the rhythm of the presentation. Timing is an art, to know what the room is reading and when to say something. In many cases, one can use humor at the start of a speech to create a positive tone and attention-grabbing effect.

It is also about content. The jokes must be concerning the topic of the speech. Unrelated jokes may either be confusing or alienating to the audience and will undermine the impact of the presentation. Including some humor that is natural with the topic adds more relevance to the message and the comprehension of the audience. An example of this would be a light-hearted personal story about the general topic, which can personalize the speaker as well as help to humanize the presentation.

There is a specific approach of self-deprecating humor, which would be good because it is humble and would help a speaker become closer to the audience. The laughter of self-depreciation allows the orator to minimize the difference that he or she feels between the audience and himself or herself. You should, however, find the right balance because too much self-effacement is not good; it destroys credibility. The important thing is to bring out a relatable imperfection without undermining your position.

A presentation can be boosted by visual humour, e.g., humorous pictures or objects. All these allow a person to have a visual relaxation in the verbal messages and mimic what the speaker is trying to explain to the audience. However, these visuals should be given in a manner that is not too dominant to the main message and does not make it look like they are trivializing.

In addition, humor must be embracing and welcoming. Make sure not to do any offensive or divisive jokes, as they can turn off a large portion of the audience. It is aimed at bringing the audience together with laughter, not to produce uneasiness and separation.

It is essential to create the kind of humor that suits you. The most important thing in this case is authenticity; the desire to soar in the air can be put to the test of any viewer and can create confusion. In addition to making, it more effective, throwing honesty into your delivery can also help you make your audience trust you.

Public speaking humor is essentially making an experience together that expands and heightens the delivery of the message. When employed in moderation, it may give a turn to a presentation and even make it entertaining as well as memorable, along with being informative. When grasped, the intricacies of humor work to be an inseparable companion to an orator and help them connect to the audience much better and communicate.

UNDERSTANDING AUDIENCE SENSITIVITIES

The fine web of personality sensitivities in modern-day public speaking is one to be threaded by the needle of a delicate artist. Learning these sensitivities goes beyond just a show of sympathy; it is a game of moves that can be used to take a speech that can be just a string of words into a strong, poignant experience.

Each audience is an individual picture of background, beliefs, and expectations. The first step that a speaker will have to take when touching this area is a careful evaluation of all these various factors. Think of the cultural implications that would affect the way people receive your message. There are ways in which cultural backgrounds may influence the perception of humor, metaphors, or even some gestures. What is very much acceptable as a joke in one culture may not be very funny or may rather be offensive in a different cultural context. Therefore, when trying to appeal to cultural sensitivities, customizing your content to suit those is of paramount importance.

Otherwise, in addition to culture, the emotional state of the audience is also a decisive factor. Get the feel of the room when you feel like delivering your speech. Are they enthusiastic and lively, or rather solemn and thoughtful because of something that has just happened? With an understanding of these emotional undercurrents, a speaker then has an opportunity to alter his tone and pacing so as to make sure that the style of the delivery hits home with the current state of mind that the audience is in.

Demographics, including age, occupation, and education level, further complicate the situation. The message that resonates with a group of young professionals might not affect the retirees. Jargon, too, used in a particular industry, may work splendidly in a roomful of those who lead and practice in the industry, but it may not work so well with a general audience. Finding the point between depth and accessibility helps in ensuring engagement among a wide variety of people.

Tenderness also applies to the personal values and beliefs that the audience has. Being a time of such intimate connections of personal beliefs to the identity of a person, a speaker has to be very careful not to offend or make people feel unwelcome. This entails a subtle sense of the subject matter, which may be sensitive or extremely personal. In considering the possible sensitivities, a speaker will be able to approach such topics in a sensitive yet respectful manner and create an atmosphere of inclusivity and goodwill.

Also, the speaker should be sensitive to the non-verbal information given off by his/ her audience. Minor changes in body movements, expressions, or even overall vibes of the room can deliver invaluable feedback. They act as a live indicator of the reception of the message, and hence, the speaker is able to make adjustments on the fly.

Lastly, the situation presented in the speech is critical. Is it a formal or an informal setting? Is it a happy or a sad event? All of these settings require a different style, and learning these subtleties will help the speech be not only decent but effective as well.

Essentially, awareness of audience sensitivities is a professional exercise that requires thinking and strategically adapting. It also makes the orators get off themselves and look through the perceptions of the people they are addressing. Through this, they will be able to develop messages that will not only be heard but also that will make them be felt, in a way that creates a connection that will go beyond the realm of the spoken word. It is this compassionate manner of communicating to the masses that delivers the excellence out of the usual to deliver an unforgettable and influential experience, which is a speech.

TIMING AND DELIVERY

In the modern way of doing interviews, timing and delivery are some of the things that are mastered to awaken an audience, making an ordinary presentation one to remember. The compounding of these two factors is rather like the tightrope walk in that coordination and balance are keys to success.

The most important aspect of giving a speech, the heartbeat, is timing, and it is much more than just following a schedule. It is the fine art of knowing when to pause, when to speed up, and when to dwell on something to make a point. Every movement, every note, and silence are choreographed to the finest detail in order to speak to the audience. A skilled orator uses timing to create suspense, to appeal to emotion, and to create interaction. However, a timely stop can say everything, so after, the audience can reflect on the burden of a phrase or look forward to the next disclosure.

On the other hand, delivery is the ipso facto through which the timing is achieved. It includes the tone of voice of the speaker, his speed, and body language. The details of an engaging delivery, which is rather lively and active, with the voice rising and falling in accordance with the natural flow of the message. One can use tone modulation to sound urgent, passionate, or calm and carry the audience along such an emotional route. Speech rhythms should not be random and should not be dreary, droning, or hectic in speed. A word at a time should be pronounced clearly to avoid the loss of information in translation.

The presence is a key factor in delivery. Body language, the nonverbal expression, supplements the verbal expression. The eye, the posture, and the gesture of a speaker either support the word which he utters or destroy its force. Authoritative posture can be portrayed; open hands initiate a connection, and looking straight into the eyes prolongs trust and connection. The movement on the stage should have a reason, and thus, one should not fidget or move around aimlessly.

That is where the power of timing and delivery strikes a speaker, making him a poor speaker as opposed to an excellent one. Please think of the crescendo of a storyline where the timing of each little detail is built up, leading to a dynamite climax, and it is done with panting breath. Or the mastery of showing nuanced information, in which one pauses strategically in order to create a picture in the mind with details, and one speaks with such a straightforward delivery that a viewer can identify with it.

Flexibility is an important skill when it comes to giving speeches. As a speaker, one needs to be responsive to the energy given off by the audience and change the timing to ensure one does not bore them. A change of tone or something of the sort, which occurs spontaneously, can take care of a lassitude of attention, or a single confusion. This agile interactivity causes a speech to become a conversation and makes it a shared experience of the speaker and the listeners.

Besides, perceptions concerning time and delivery can be shaped by cultural situations. What is thought to be a good breather may be thought of as hesitation in another culture. It is therefore a cultural requirement that such a speaker must be sensitive to adapt the approach to the audience.

Finally, the mastery of time and presentation is the key to effective speaking skills. More practice, intuition, and an openness to sharpen one's work, work by work, are all needed. By putting these elements together in a perfectly harmonized combination, a speaker has an opportunity to exercise the power of words and inform, inspire, influence, and leave an unforgettable impact on the audience.

AVOIDING OVERUSE

When it comes to the field of public speaking, there is always the temptation to overindulge in some specific figures of speech or even in some aspects of style. The problem that normally plagues speakers is that they tend to be excessive with their techniques, and techniques that, when used sensibly, can benefit their message, can eliminate the power thereof when overused. This sensation must meet this subtle balance and must find in itself an awareness and meticulous practice in preserving the whole and transparency of speech.

An example of this is the use of repetition, which is a very effective weapon in a speech. It can emphasize a statement, fix an idea in the minds of the hearers, and give it a rhythmical sound in the speech. Nevertheless, excessive use results in boredom and a lack of interest. Listeners could get tuned out, their attentions fading since they are left with the impression that they are being bombarded with something redundant over what is supposed to be reinforcement. The art to it is to be able to know when to repeat to make an emphasis and when to leave the message alone.

Likewise, special vocabulary or jargon may be a boomerang. It is capable of conferring credibility and proving skill, but it may be jeopardized if it is applied too frequently. People who do not know the terms being used may feel left out; they have a grey mist covering them with unknown words. One has to assess the familiarity of the audience with the subject matter and vary with language, and this should be clear and inclusive.

Use of humor in a speech is one of the things that needs to be done with moderation. A good joke will help to release some tension, make the speaker likable, and sustain the interest of the audience. However, excessive humor may take away the seriousness of the message, and the audience will not be able to identify the real motive of the speech. Besides, not everything that one considers funny will be deemed as such by everyone, and too much humor may appear either irrelevant or noisy.

Anecdotes and personal stories can be used to give a very vivid picture and make the information more personified. Nevertheless, excessive use of personal stories may take away some attention from the general idea of the speech and cause it to be too subjective. The speaker's experience should only be used to unite the audience with the subject, not the entirety of the discussion.

Well-adapted visual aids promote retention as well as comprehension of information. However, excess slides or graphics end up blinding the listeners, and he can barely follow what the speaker is saying. The trick here is to apply the visual aids in a limited amount, with everything accompanied to relieve as opposed to fighting with the spoken word.

To prevent being too commonplace in rhetoric, the concept of mindfulness and being intentional should be applied. It entails close attention to the audience, the situation, and the essence of the message that one wants to convey. Being aware of how frequently certain elements are used or used in regard to the specific situation, a speaker would be able to keep the attention of his/her audience, and better make the message memorable and therefore impactful. It aims to add more to the show, rather than to cover the actual message with the excessive use of style.

CHAPTER 11

Cultural Sensitivity

UNDERSTANDING CULTURAL DIFFERENCES

Effective cultural mobility is a leadership quality in the public speaking world that goes beyond communication ability. Culture consists of values, beliefs, practices, and social norms that a group of people share, and affect how they communicate and their interpretation. When speakers are trying to communicate with varied segments of the population, then knowledge of such cultural discretion becomes a key in communicating words that reach and relate to people.

Think of a situation where the culture of an audience and your own differ in a big way. The words you use, the gestures that you use, and the intonation of your voice can have different implications and have different meanings. What one ego might learn to consider aggressive and bold may be seen as rude and aggressive in another culture. On the same level, the use of humour can be a very effective means of engagement, but jokes that may bring laughter in one culture fail to excite or are even offensive in another.

Public speaking in a multicultural context also requires a certain sensitivity to the differences. It requires the speaker to adjust their content and delivery to correlate with the culture that their audience is expecting of them. The first part of this will be research and preparation, and knowing the target culture's social history may be of great help in knowing their values and style of communication. It entails putting into consideration things like formality, hierarchy, and individualism versus collectivism, which can go a long way in affecting the reception of messages.

As an example, in collectivism-oriented cultures, like most of the Asian and Latin American cultures, a public speaker may focus on the community, collaboration, and community good. By comparison, messages with more of an emphasis placed on individual success and personal independence may be better received by viewers with a more individualistic culture, including the United States or Western Europe.

Another important thing is non-verbal communication in eliminating cultural differences. Movements of the body, eye contact, and gestures may be extremely different in different cultures and may strengthen or weaken what the speaker says. In certain cultures, when people look directly in the eye, they are showing confidence and sincerity, or in other cultures, this may be viewed as intrusive or disrespectful. Speakers need to understand these non-verbal communication strategies in order to avoid losing their message along the way in translation.

Culture also includes a significant language aspect. Although I may use English as a lingua franca in most international contexts, one can improve clarity and connection by understanding the language nuances and idiomatic expressions that may be appealing to other cultural groups. Removal of language jargon and colloquialisms, as well as good knowledge of all colloquialisms, can support the core message so that all participants of the audience can share it.

After all, the objective of learning about the cultural differences when it comes to spoken messaging is the creation of an atmosphere of inclusiveness and respect. Respecting and being sensitive to cultural diversity, the speakers are able to create rapport, gain credibility, and create an environment where everyone is willing and feels appreciated to talk. This not only helps the speaker to improve the effectiveness of the message they deliver, but also enriches the experience of the audience, resulting in improved cross-exchange of ideas and perspectives.

With increasing trends of globalization that are also simultaneously erasing geographical borders, the power to communicate cross-culturally has become a significant issue in the world where we live. It is an ability to enable the speakers to cross cultural boundaries, reach audiences with different backgrounds, and motivate the world to change.

COMMUNICATING ACROSS CULTURES

In a globalized world where physical boundaries become permeable and the exchange of thoughts has no geographical boundaries; to be a good speaker, one has to understand the cultural diversity of the people subtly. Contemporary speaking is not only planning a speech in front of the audience; it is a way of overcoming the distances between differences brought by different cultures. The complexity of the dance, which should include verbal and non-verbal communication, is complicated even further when a person goes out on the global stage.

Consider how to talk in a room with many people having various backgrounds, and different environments precondition a particular set of cultural norms, values, and expectations. Such is becoming a more and more typical situation in the now-globalized world. These are the keys to the question of the above issue: how can one communicate effectively across cultures without demeaning and denying these differences?

Awareness is the initial process in this multifaceted process. What must be understood is that gestures, expressions, and even silence can mean different things in various cultures. A nod may mean that one has agreed to something when applied in one culture, but in another culture, it may only mean that one is just listening to something. Thus, knowing the cultural background of your audience will become a critical point. By watching and studying what is acceptable in a culture, research can give priceless information regarding how your information may be accepted.

Language is one of the most powerful tools, but it can be a barrier. When it comes to multilingual contexts, clarity and simplicity must dictate words. It is important to avoid using idioms and jargon, which may not be translatable very well. Rather, use such universal terms and concepts that are not limited by the language. Also, it is worth remembering the tempo and tone to deliver the message in order to affect the understanding and response.

There is also non-verbal communication, which is also referred to as the silent language, and it is equally important. Warmth, confidence, and sincerity can be detected via eye contact and body language, as well as facial expressions, yet they can be mistaken. As an excerpt, eye contact is valued as a symbol of confidence in most Western cultures, but is taken as offensive in some Asian cultures. Knowledge of these nuances proves to be paramount in making non-verbal communication support and not negate the verbal one.

In addition, expectations and acceptance of a speech by an audience are characterized by the cultural background of a listening community. Some cultures prefer listening to stories and appeals to emotion, and others prefer facts and rational approaches. You can turn your message more compelling by changing and matching the combination and formats of your message to suit these tendencies. This flexibility is not merely respectful, but it also predisposes to success in communicating with different people.

Creating an inclusive and receptive environment is also the top priority. The promotion of questions and a discussion would result in a two-way communication in which the issue of cultural barriers can be discussed and resolved. This communication leads to a feeling of belonging and understanding another person and turns a one-way talk into a two-way interaction.

In conclusion, multicultural communication is not only about the language; we have to talk about empathy, respect, and the desire to comprehend the point of view, which may not be similar to ours. It means acknowledging the fact that each member of the audience has a part of their culture to bring to the table, and as a speaker, we must respect and utilize that diversity. We are really improving our speaking skills, being more sensitive and more enlightened world citizens, all the time, as we are immersing ourselves in the maze of international communication.

RESPECTFUL LANGUAGE USE

Under the conditions of the modern world of public speaking, the advantages of words are much larger than those of communication.

Language is a means of power and a connector between different points of view. Therefore, the crucial aspect of selecting the words carefully is essential as it helps to make the message that is conveyed not only clear, but also respectful and inclusive.

The respectful language used in public speech is all about internalizing the worth of each person sitting in the audience. It is also about how words can leave an impression on the audience and how they should not make them feel like they are outside the picture. This involves a responsible initiative to have a picture of the cultural, social, and personal background of the audience.

One of the things included in respectful language is the lack of stereotyping and generalizations. They can even be caused unconsciously, leading to misunderstandings and reinforcing preconceptions. Rather than this, speakers ought to employ the use of language that recognizes the uniqueness of an individual, or avoid generic statements where what is being said may not necessarily be true about everybody. Such a sensitivity to diversity can be useful in the process of establishing a rapport with the audience, as it allows them to demonstrate that the speaker is respectful of and values their diverse experiences.

The other important aspect is inclusiveness in language, where they come up with words that do not marginalize or exclude any group of people. This implies sensitivity to gender-neutral language and a lack of presumption about roles or identities, various capabilities, and backgrounds. Take, for instance, the word, oh, instead of using the word, chairman, you could use the word, chairperson, or chair, and this can make a lot of difference in ensuring that everyone feels heard and respected in the audience.

It is also essential to consider the tone to demonstrate respect. The tone that a speaker uses can be very warm and welcoming, or it can distance and make a person go on the defensive. Respectful tone is empathetic, understanding, and patient, and the environment makes the audience members feel safe to connect and participate. This is especially relevant when speaking about delicate issues where people are more prone to be emotionally charged, and misunderstandings are more likely to happen.

Besides, the language used in the speech ought to be determined by the situation of the speech. What would be suitable in an informal setting may be taken to be rude in an official one. It's important to realize how subtle the occasion is; you need to be aware of how the audience figures out what the expectations are with the language used, because that helps to make it right and respectable.

The other constituent of respectful communication is active listening. When they pay attention to audience feedback and the audience responses, speakers are able to manipulate language and approach, which they use during the conversation in real-time to align their message better with the needs of the audience. This shows that effective communication and respect for the views of the audience are needed.

In the end, the use of respectful language is concerned with establishing positive interaction and understanding differences. It is an ongoing development of learning and self-reflection because speakers then aim to become more effective in the process of communication. With the progressive nature of the public sphere, respectful vocabulary is no longer a matter of courtesy but a requirement to convey meaningful and effective communication.

By righting the use of respect in language before anything, we not only become effective communicators, but we also ensure a culture that encourages harmonization of our societies. Such a style of public speaking will help every voice to be heard and appreciated, which will lead to effective dialogue and respect for each other in the future.

GLOBAL PERSPECTIVES ON PUBLIC SPEAKING

Speaking in public is a cross-cultural, cross-societal activity with its thread connecting the different cultures and societies all over the world. Even though the general purpose is communication, certain specifics of the process of public speaking are very different and depend on surrounding cultural norms, historical backgrounds, and social priorities. The skill of successful oration not only depends on the choice of words delivered but also on the ability to know the cultural background of the listeners, which can literally make the difference of not just a word but an echo of a speech.

Direct/assertive style is also characteristic of the way people normally speak in most Western cultures. One of the recommended aspects of speakers is to look in the eye, gesture, and have a clear and confident tone. This is based on the idea of the significance of individualism and self-expression. The readers expect some logical form, some sequential organization of the arguments, and some data and evidence. With the help of expertise, experience, and being able to create rational discourse, the credibility of a speaker is often derived.

On the other hand, public speaking in most eastern cultures is more indirect, and the speaker is expected to place stress on harmony and respect. The orator can become more modest in tone and tends to underplay his or her role in favor of the group or society. Proverbs, stories, and analogies are commonly used as they strongly appeal to the audiences who are used to learning with stories. Authority of the speaker is sometimes created by the fact that he can prove that he is a wise and sensitive man, not a straightforward, assertive one.

Public speaking may also be collective in African cultures, as a part and parcel of the oral tradition that was transmitted through generations of Africans. Storytelling can be a very strong means, where it is not only used as a means to inform but also to amuse and educate. Chanting, or singing, is highly important, along with the important musicality and rhythm of the speech, and the involvement of the audience through the senses. The dynamics between the speaker and the listeners is the most important aspect here, and the emphasis is on creating this common experience.

The culture of Latin America can also create a vivid demonstration of the topic in its way of speaking. A big part of it is emotion and expression, and speakers will often use their total body to convey their message. The listeners are also regarded as participants, and the distinction between them and the speaker is also fluid, and the two can interact and engage with one another. It focuses on the dynamic atmosphere that is created when the audience reflects the energy of the speaker.

Most Middle Eastern cultures regard public speaking as part of their traditions and are usually affected by religious oratory instruments. The speaker plays the role of inspiring and motivating; most times, they rely on historical or religious texts to give depth to what they are saying. The expressions of good word use and poetics are typical, and the beauty of the spoken word dominates. There is a central respect for the audience and orientation to cultural norms, and stress is placed on humility and sacredness.

All these points of view in culture contribute different tastes to the art of public speech, emphasizing the various manners of communication and human connectivity. Becoming aware of such differences not only makes us appreciate diversity in global communication but also helps us step up our game in terms of communicating effectively with different audiences and different backgrounds. In today's ever more globalized world, the skill of adapting your public speaking style to different people, and being able to reach them and gain their attention, no longer remains a good skill to have, but a necessity.

CHAPTER 12

Improving with Feedback

SEEKING CONSTRUCTIVE CRITICISM

As the world constantly evolves on the stage of public speaking, perfection and sophistication are a journey indeed. When constructive criticism is sought, another of the most powerful tools in the journey is achieved. This is an activity that may be intimidating, but it is a mandatory practice in developing and growing as a speaker. It is an active form of seeking feedback that is not only smart but also actionable, so that speakers can develop it as an art form.

The first measure in accepting constructive criticism is always to adopt a mind that is learning and growing. It must require such appreciation that regardless of how gifted a person might be, he/she can always improve. Such openness preconditions the receipt of feedback productively and helpfully.

Constructive criticism can be described as enhancing and developing the skills one has. There is a difference between negative criticism that is disheartening and destructive, and constructive criticism, which only looks at areas of improvement rather than strengths. It gives an objective opinion urging speakers to persist with efforts, as it also speaks of areas that could require improvement.

It is important to find proper sources that will help one in both seeking and retaining positive criticism. Not every feedback is equally triggered, and being able to choose the voices to listen to is also an art. Experienced peers, audience, and other trusted mentors have much to contribute to the field through the disclosure of their expertise and knowledge based on experience. Their responses are usually subtle and astute, and their viewpoint can be called both informed and constructive.

To handle the feedback, one has to be open-minded and anxious to hear other opinions. These include active listening, probing questions, and contemplating what is being said. It also helps to separate the subjective opinions and objective observations, according to which it is better to concentrate changes.

Searching for constructive criticism must be a back-and-forth process, whereby each feedback session is progressive towards later stages of competence. Once feedback is received, implementing the suggestions therein and noting the effect it will have on the performance later is vital. This feedback loop and implementation process will lead to self-improvement and will enable the speaker to create a more polished and efficient delivery.

Further, constructive criticism is not only concerned with areas of improvement, but it is also concerned with the areas of strength, identification of strength, and strengthening them. Knowing what is good about the way a presentation looks can give confidence and form a basis for constructing new skills. When the technique of positive reinforcement is added with some constructive suggestions, an equilibrium is brought forth, which will encourage the speakers to continue their proceedings.

And finally, the quest for constructive criticism is part and parcel of the quest to become a better speaker in public. It takes boldness, humility, and personal development. Speakers may achieve their goal of becoming effective presenters by simply looking for and welcoming feedback about their presentation performance. This helps them make a phenomenal impact on the audience instead of having their performance have no resonance. That way, constructive criticism can be conceived as a driving force towards evolution and perfection with respect to the world of public speaking.

ANALYZING AUDIENCE REACTIONS

The art of recognizing and deciphering the emotional responses of a target audience is a crucial element of the contemporary world of the art of effectively communicating with people through the medium of speech. To have an idea of how an audience has received their message enables a speaker to adjust a given delivery during a presentation to keep the listener interested and, on a message,-connected line.

By getting on the stage, the first thing a speaker should tune in to is the minor signs that the audience gives. These are the non-verbal clues made up of a facial expression, body language, and the energy in the room. These signals may be detected not only with attentiveness but also with a great sense of how humans behave.

One of the most distressing cues to the reception of a speech is the facial expression. An ocean of nodding heads and wide grins can signal the fact that the speech was agreeable and interesting; frowning faces or a dead stare can indicate confusion or the loss of interest. A speaker should be keen on such responses as they could be used to slow the pace, change the tone, or even the subject matter to fit the needs of the audience properly.

The audience's reaction is further enriched with body language. Crossed arms or leaning forward can reflect different attitudes, interests, or disagreements. A speaker who knows how to read such signs may change the way he is doing and reestablish the attention and trust of the audience, maybe adding some more relatable anecdotes or explaining some complicated things.

Another very important thing to consider is the collective energy of an audience. Interactive listeners can be dynamic, but they can also have a sense of energy (being attentively silent or engaging in interactions). In contrast, an audience that is not attentive may also need the speaker to match the tone of the discussion against a more energetic approach that may include alternating the tone of the voice or injections of engaging elements to re-attract attention.

It is also important to listen to auditory feedback. The rhythm of applause, how and when the audience laughs, or the mere sound of whispered conversations to and fro may yield whatever information as to the effect upon the audience. A perfectly-timed break after a poignant remark may enable one to think, or a comical joke can dispel the tension and create mutual bonding.

Further, demographics of audiences are influential factors as they determine reactions. Studying the cultural, social, and professional background of the audience will enable a speaker to decide on the language, examples, and references to use. Since these factors can be adjusted to suit the context of understanding the audience, they will not only increase relatability but also show regard and respect.

The analysis of the audience has come to have new layers due to the digital era. Online platforms provide interesting problems and opportunities for speakers to reach their audience. In this kind of setting, it is essential to track the chat conversation, the emoticon response, and the online activity report. A speaker who is adept at working such digital cues will be able to appear, even behind a screen, to be in full presence.

After all, the role of audience analysis is a very dynamic exercise, and it needs a combination of observation, empathy, and flexibility. Allowing such a speaker to perfect the art, he can turn a speech into a conversation, create a rapport that is beyond words. With frequent practice of learning how to read and react to cues given by the audience, speakers will be able to make sure that the message communicated by them not only reaches their audience but also cuts deep and can invoke a strong feeling, so it is memorable.

IMPLEMENTING CHANGES

The art of public speaking is a very dynamic field, and adaptation and general evolution are key to success. The delivery and the content of these speakers are changes that need to be made as the speakers attempt to relate to different audiences. This involves a lot of sensitivity both towards the self and the audience, and it also involves the capacity to change.

When trying to make changes in one's speaking strategy, the best first step is to analyze oneself. This includes an analysis based on previous performances, strengths, and weaknesses, as well as what needs to be done in order to be better. In this way, speakers will be able to identify the areas that could use improvement, like the way they speak, body movements, or the way they have organized their message. This soul searching is a precursor to good change.

The audience should also be understood in terms of its changing needs and expectations. Speakers have to be aware of these changes in a world where cultures have contexts and social values are variable and changing very quickly. Such knowledge enables one to target the audience in terms of content and style to reach more deeply into the hearts of the audience. Be it an attempt to reach the industry specialists or a general audience, the ability to deliver a message in a manner that would resonate with the interests and concerns of users is imperative.

The involvement of new technologies may be significant as well in introducing changes in public speaking. The digital era provides a set of tools that can help deliver presentations, such as complex presentation software and interactive fields that can get the audience involved in the process in real-time. These technologies can be combined to allow the speakers to work in a more immersive and interesting way, attract attention as well, and promote a higher level of understanding.

Also, feedback is a precious asset in the process of effecting changes. They can be in the form of constructive criticism by fellow peers, coaches, or even audience members, which gives one points that they may not have noticed during their speech. Having an open mind and receiving such feedback can help the speakers improve their techniques and style. It is by passing through this process of iteration that speakers are ensured that they can be the master and remain applicable in their area of occupation.

Successful change implementation is achieved through the application of practical exercises and repetition. The speakers are able to gain confidence and fluency by exercising new methods in a simulated environment. Such rehearsals provide a possibility to practice various styles and methods in order to evaluate how performance can be built and then to enter the stage when it is time to give speeches. Moreover, it is possible to archive these sessions and record them, as it would allow speakers to obtain lots of useful visual and audible feedback and see what needs to be improved.

By nature, change can prove to be intimidating. Yet, the readiness to leave the comfort zone is what may bring changes and enhancements to a great extent. Making changes in the process of public speaking is not a matter of trying to drop the image of a speaker but instead improving on it through intelligent metamorphosis. With the change as a friend in the pocket, a speaker becomes flexible and dynamic enough to improve their art and perfect it with each lesson.

Change implementation in public speaking will in the end be a learning and reconnaissance voyage. It demands a balance of self-reflection, perception of the audience, integrating technology, and outreach to constant learning. With such efforts, speakers will not just be able to respond to the needs of today, they will also be able to predict and pre-condition decisions of the future and still have their messages relevant even many years after the last word has been uttered.

CONTINUOUS IMPROVEMENT

Speaking is an art that keeps on improving, and it requires one to improve and adjust continually. The core idea of this process is continuous improvement, the methodology that prompts the speakers to analyze the experience and improve the level and methods constantly. This chapter explores the leadership strategies that the speaker must adopt in order to be relevant and effective in presentations.

The first thing is to realize that every speaking engagement can lead to improvement. One thing that speakers need to do is to cultivate an attitude of seeing each presentation as an educational exercise. This will enable them to know their strengths and weaknesses. The tendency to self-reflection will help the speakers determine particular aspects of their delivery, including vocal variety, body language, and interaction with the audience, which could be developed upon.

The process of continuous improvement includes feedback as a part of it. Some constructive comments from peers, mentors, or the audience can be of great help, and their ideas can give solid hints on how well a speaker performs. It is necessary to receive feedback open-mindedly and be ready to consider it. Presenters are able to create a base of persons to whom one can pass on an honest and thorough critique. This outside view identifies blind areas that the speaker may be unaware of, and precise improvements can be made.

In addition to feedback, speakers ought to be keen on learning opportunities that can enhance their knowledge and skills. Practicing through workshops, taking courses in public speaking, or being a part of the speaking clubs, such as Toastmasters, can provide a systemized process of training. These sites also offer an encouraging community in which the speakers can test new procedures and get on-the-spot feedback.

Besides, the age of the digital world presents a vast range of materials that can facilitate the progressive development of public speaking. Webinars, online courses, and podcasts are capable of exposing the speakers to new practices and international approaches. Viewing the variety of content helps speakers to open their appeal to the various styles and solutions in the domain of effective speaking.

Recording and reviewing self-speeches is another very effective activity that can be used to make continuous improvement. Video recordings are an objective resource that enables the speakers to see themselves from a third-party perspective of their performance. An overview of such tapes will allow speakers to learn what can be improved: pacing, clarity, and interaction with the audience. This self-evaluation promotes the enhancement of deeper knowledge towards the personal habits and trends in support of deliberate analysis.

Continuous improvement also involves experimentation. Presenters are not supposed to be afraid to experiment with new ideas and methods. Some ideas are so invaluable as to be revolutionary: using storytelling, multimedia, the organization of a presentation, and so on, can come as discoveries in their effectiveness, too, once you start playing. Being innovative may give a breath to the presentations and make the style of the speaker interesting and new.

Lastly, it can be motivated by having definite objectives to guide them in the effort of seeking constant improvement. Such objectives need to be realistic, measurable, and should meet the bigger picture that the speaker is aiming to achieve. Through monitoring and rewarding accomplishments, the speakers will be able to feel accomplished and motivated.

The process of never-ending improvement when it comes to taking to the podium is, in a way, never-ending learning and adaptation. The attainment of new levels and a closer connection to an audience is possible with feedback, knowledge-seeking, and a culture of experimentation, which are essential to the continuous improvement of fluent speakers. This dedication to improvement means their message will always have an impression and a meaning in any speaking situation.

CHAPTER 13

Advanced Speaking Techniques

MASTERING VOCAL VARIETY

Vocal variety is an important skill in the world of present-day public speaking. Knowledge is important in a verge, and the utilization of language is supposed to be where words are important, but the deeper connection to the audience is through vocalization. The fossil of vocal variety, which is the expressive use of tone, pitch, volume, and pace in the delivery of speech, is the faux pas that transforms the monologue into a verbal symphony.

A speaker who speaks in a monotone is something to imagine. The lines can be very deep, but if there is no variety, they do not make any waves, do not cause an effect on the emotions of the audience, and do not draw their attention to it. On the contrary, a listener who is skillful in controlling tone of voice is capable of making people feel compassion, passion, or reflection, and to get them closer to the centre of a message.

The first element to discuss is tone, which is the emotional quality of the voice. It indicates the attitude of the speaker, and it could be warm, authoritative, or urgent. When talking about a very serious subject, the speaker will use a serious tone; in a humorous story, a lighter and conversational tone could be used. The speakers can influence the tone and thus direct the audience to the needed emotion, which becomes the connection that works beyond words.

Another level of participation is the frequency of the voice and pitch. The usage of different pitches assists in clarifying important points and holding the attention of the audience. When a speaker is using a higher pitch, he or she may be showing excitement or surprise, but using a lower pitch, he or she may be showing seriousness or confidence. Articulate speakers will employ a variation of pitch to elicit essential points of the speech, and the delivery will make the speaker's message vital to the listener.

Loudness is a very strong command-employing audio and is called volume. Strong volume may shock an audience into being attentive, while a mumble can lure them, establishing a close feel. The art of volume is strategic in that it not only conveys emphasis of critical positions but also provides drama and emotion, making a speech an experience in sound.

The pace completes the four members of the quartet of vocal variety, the speed of talking or speaking. The fast speed may be used to show urgency or excitement, whereas the slow speed will provide time to think and reduce stress. Experienced speakers are aware of how to change the flow of speech to correspond with the needed part of the speech, accelerating when they need to go to a climax of the speech and slowing down when they need to allow the main ideas to register.

The art of the use of vocal variations is one of natural incorporation into the style of a speaker. It is not about dramatic reinventions or overdone delivery, but about not being out of balance to support the message, but not letting it be out-focused. Relevant measures in acquiring this skill involve doing vocal exercises, speech recording, and getting feedback.

Finally, it is a matter of sincerity when it comes to learning how to develop vocal variety. It involves the application of the voice as a tool to express the true emotion and purpose so that the audience feels that the speaker is talking to him/her. By mastering such a technique, orators bring words into the life of conversation, and their impression on listeners is unforgettable. In modern-day public speaking, vocal variability is not just one of the methods. Still, it is the pulsation of good communication that gives words life and opens the imagination of people in any place.

ADVANCED STORYTELLING METHODS

The craft of storytelling in the field of modern oratory has become a complex maze of tricks aimed at delivering the highest-rate effects and sparking the audience's interest at a deeper mental level. Speakers are under pressure to use more sophisticated ways of telling the story because of the sophistication that characterizes modern-day communications, ensuring that a presentation is composed in such a way that it includes elements of emotion, arouses the senses, and provides a form of participation in the presentation.

Emotional resonance is the name of the game behind all these sophisticated techniques. Speakers are currently weaving tales to access universal human experiences and portray a plethora of emotions that would include joy and inspiration, as well as empathy and introspection. When speakers develop characters and situations that apply to the lives of the audience members with regard to their own lives and desired goals, they shape that specific connection, and it will last long after the talk is over. This emotional appeal is further enhanced through pacing and tone, which gives the speakers the ability to take their audience members on an emotional journey through the ups and downs of their story.

One of the crucial aspects of contemporary storytelling is the use of the sensory experience, which brings the abstract ideas alive, making them tangible. Speechwriters can create a mental movie by using descriptive terms that engage the senses. Describing things using senses means providing a more immersive and memorable mental picture. These physical details anchor the reader's imagination with sights, smells, and sounds of a busy market, as well as the soft rustling of trees in a more distant forest, bringing this story closer to the readers and making it more effective and memorable. These sensory experiences can also be reinforced using visual aids, i.e., the use of images and videos that make the result a truly multi-dimensional narrative that is also very appealing to the attention of the audience.

Interactivity has become a feature of mature storytelling, where audiences have been challenged to participate as protagonists in the drama. Speakers establish a co-creative environment by polling the audience, asking rhetorical questions, and obtaining immediate feedback. This not only contributes to increased interaction but also to the empowerment of the audience, which feels like an important part of the story's development. Interactive storytelling dissolves the historical boundary between a speaker and an audience, making people feel communal and connected.

More than that, the incorporation of technology in storytelling has disrupted the storytelling processes by providing more advanced tools that can expand the scope of conventional narratives. AR, VR, and immersive simulations enable the speakers to develop lively, involving spaces to carry the viewer to the center of the narration. These up-to-date technologies not only impress but also teach, in that they also offer learning experiences that are interesting and educational.

There are metaphors and symbolism that are used to create several levels of high-brow storytelling to allow audiences to delve deeper into a framework that explains complex ideas in the context of something familiar. It is through the use of the combination of abstract and relatable themes in the story that speakers can convey deeper wisdom utilizing a language that is relatable yet provoking. Such an approach can stimulate viewers to analyze the idea and reflect on it in their own way, which makes the reception wider and deeper.

Finally, recent developments in modern-day storytelling techniques in public speaking are aimed at overcoming the rigidity of standard narratives and, instead, producing a very detailed picture full of feel, smell, and engagement. With the implementation of these new methods, the speaker is able to create a passionate narrative that can connect with the audience in a way that can influence them to change the world, telling their own story towards a sense of establishment of a difference in the realm of communication.

THE ART OF PERSUASION

The power to convince in the sphere of a public speaker turns out to be like a well-tuned tool. It is not just about giving the facts or telling the opinions. Still, it is about telling a story that would connect with the audience on another level, something that would make them accept, take, or take action on the ideas that are being given. The art of persuasion is an art that necessitates a fine touch of reason, appeal, and merit.

Knowledge of the audience is what persuasion is based on. You have to probe the psychology of the audience, be keen on understanding what they care about, what they believe, and what they want. This is what the persuasive argument is constructed on. It is like an artist selecting a palette that will bring out what he or she wants the viewer to expect. When the speaker knows what motivates people and what the audience is interested in, it is easy to create the message in a manner that appeals to their preconceptions and ambitions.

A persuasive speech depends on organization. It has a good start that attracts the attention of the reader and precedes the main message. It is the key to opening the mind of the audience, and it should be grasping and relatable. The speaker should now give a defined thesis, a point of purpose that is a peg of the whole discourse. This thesis should be justified by the illogical aspects, which should be interlinked with the evidence and back-up examples, which add substance to the advantages it raises.

Emotion is the key to persuasion. The good speaker should know how to make the audience engage with the emotions awakened and how to convey these emotions using either storytelling, bright images, or animated speech. Emotion forms a bond, a bridge between the speaker and the audience, that would not be possible to create with logic alone. It is the appeal to emotion, and this can usually influence the audience, making them take action or even change their way of thinking.

But when there is no credibility behind the emotion, it isn't very sensible. The presenter has to produce ethos, the reliance on credibility and power. This is done by displaying knowledge, showing qualifications, and demonstrating honesty. To be humble to the message of the speaker, the audience should think that he is sincere and competent. This is because credibility is the foundation of the persuasive argument, and it alone can make or break the most passionate and reasoned appeals.

The art of persuasion does not only lie with what is said in the speech, but also with how it is said. The way the speaker talks, his gestures, and his presence work, thus making the message very convincing. Dynamic presentation of a well-built argument can take it further and make it even more compelling and memorable. The speaker should also monitor the reactions of the audience to be able to readjust their strategy every so often, so as to ensure the audience remains engaged and also effective.

Public speaking is an ongoing learning experience that requires learning how to persuade. It involves a sensitive self-understanding, an understanding of others, and an art of holding up the threads of logic, sentiment, and plausibility in a unity. Whenever persuasion is successfully done with deftness and subtlety, it can be an effective weapon, and it can effect not only change, but thought on an immense scale.

ENGAGING THE SENSES

In the scope of the art of public speaking, the skill of touching the senses can make a relatively good talk something remarkable. Using all five senses of sight, sound, smell, taste, and touch, a speaker may make his setting multisensory, and the environment will attract attention, evoke emotions, and impress the memory.

The visual aspect tends to be the most accessible mode of capturing an audience. Rendering clear pictures through the use of visual descriptions and the gift of language can give a picture to the listeners in their minds, enabling them to visualize whatever narrative a speaker is developing. The speaker may talk about the dazzling colors of the sunset, or the elaborate design of a tapestry, or the very smooth design of a modern gadget, and each emphasizes a richness in the story. These descriptions can be reinforced and improve comprehension and memorization when used together with well-designed visual aids such as slides or props.

Another strong asset that the speaker owns is the use of sound. The voice expectations can be passionate, anxious, or relaxed, and the tone, pitch, and rhythm of the speaker's voice can present this. The pause at the right moment may add more suspense or intensity in emphasizing somewhere in saying, between vocal dynamics, one can keep the listeners awake and not bored. Also, some music or sound effects can be used to give a mood, or they can support a theme and make a speech more of an experience.

Perhaps more so, the use of the sense of smell, which is less often utilised, can be far more evocative. A smell can take an audience on another trip and can induce feelings and memories by telling them about a smell. When speaking about the aroma of freshly baked bread, the fresh scent of pine forests, or the stagnant fish smell of the ocean, a detail can be used to bring diversity into a story. To further foster a strong multisensory connection, in some scenarios, like workshops or interactions, an appeal to actual scents may be made.

Taste is also capable of being a powerful incitement of memories and feelings, as is smell. On the one hand, it is harder to apply directly in a speech, but a speaker can, however, use descriptive language to get an idea of the taste and feel. Telling about the taste of citrus, the flavor of sweet strawberries, and what it feels like to be sipping a spiced latte can dip the imagination of the audience and bring it closer to the reader or listener.

Touch, which is not taken seriously most of the time, can help to increase the feeling of connection between the audience and the speaker. The quality of items can be described, for example, by how velvet is soft to the touch, how a piece of sandpaper feels coarse, and how much a smooth piece of marble feels cool to the touch on a countertop. In interactive contexts, it is good to see others develop an interest in an activity or event by manipulating items or materials.

These sensory details have to be employed with consideration and purpose. A speaker must be true to himself so that sensory images do not take away the main message but augment it. Vivid appeal to the audience's senses is not only a useful tool for a speaker but also a way to help evolve the atmosphere of the experience. Such a strategy can make any public speaking not just the transfer of the information but a memorable and exuberant experience that will leave a significant mark on the hearts of the people lucky to listen.

CHAPTER 14

The Future of Public Speaking

EMERGING TRENDS

In a fast-changing world of contemporary public speaking, there are some of these changes that are emerging to change the way speaker address audiences and how they deliver their messages. With more and more globalization and interconnection of people, the art of public speaking must be able to adapt to the new technologies and changes in the cultures, as well as the expectations of the audience.

It is undoubtedly one of the most important shifts; we now have digital tools incorporated into the presentations. Speakers are no longer restricted to physical stages due to the emergence of virtual platforms. Rather, by means of webinars, live streams, and online conferences, they can target global audiences. Such transformation presupposes that the speakers acquire new skills, like handling the virtual meeting software, interacting with viewers using the chat facilities of the platform, and maintaining a vigorous online presence. It is essential in the realm of online communication because people define their oratory competence as equal to old, proven skills.

Moreover, a change is happening in the content of public speaking. Nowadays, people are not satisfied with reading information only; they want to hear the stories to which they can relate. The current shift towards storytelling is done in the name of authenticity and connection. Speakers increasingly use personal anecdotes, relatable stories, and emotional appeals to establish a connection with the audience. It not only attracts attention but also memorizes the message.

The second trend is the focus on the inclusivity and diversity of the public speaking activity. Being in a more socially conscious world, speakers have to remember and address different opinions. These are language considerations, representation, and accessibility. Presenters have become more aware of building spaces that are not those where voices are not heard or respect is not given. The same trend can be observed in the rising interest in the speaker representatives of different backgrounds who introduce new perspectives into the discussion and expand it.

Technology has remained a central element in the present public speaking. Augmented reality (AR) and virtual reality (VR) have also started to feature in presentations, providing in-depth experiences that fascinate viewers. Such technologies enable presenters to develop engaging and interactive environments where the delivery and reception of information is redetermined. Also, the application of data analytics is giving the information that helps speakers understand how the audience follows the presentation, and the speakers can adjust their presentation better to match the needs and interests of the audience.

The emergence of social media has contributed to public speaking as well because there is a disconnection between old-time speeches and online content. Instagram, Twitter, and TikTok are new platforms that allow the speakers to present their messages and cover broad audiences. The result of this trend has been the emergence of so-called micro-speakers who have no traditional stage but who can still make an impact on thousands of people by posting small videos and getting their message out through short posts.

Finally, a particular emphasis on sustainability and ethics in terms of public speaking has also emerged. Today, speakers are also supposed to tackle issues concerning environmental responsibility and social justice. This is part of a wider social movement toward being conscious and making ethical choices, and this is the way speakers need to focus their message on these preferences.

These new trends are constantly developed in this dynamic world where the ability of public speakers is evolving, and they improvise their ways of skill and strategy to respond to the evolving needs of the audience all over the world. This is clearly the skill to be able to manoeuvre in this changing world when one seeks to make a difference by the force of the spoken word.

THE ROLE OF AI AND TECHNOLOGY

In the continually changing world of public speaking, the introduction of artificial intelligence (AI) and technology is a groundbreaking phenomenon, reinventing how speakers can reach their audiences. The contemporary age of public communication is characterized by the unprecedented access to technological tools contributing to the preparation and delivery of speeches.

The advent of AI has become an essential concept relating to the sphere of public speaking. It provides talkers with sophisticated content building, analysis, and presentation tools. As an example, the AI-powered venues are able to help the speakers design their talk, proposing to them on the pertinence of the content, honing their expressions, and even foreseeing the response of the audience. Such channels provide feedback and tips on current issues and successful message delivery based on analyzing huge data volumes, so that orators can customize their messages depending on the needs.

In addition, technology enables rehearsing, and speakers can train using AI-based feedback systems. Such systems grade them not only by evaluating the content but also based on the style of delivery, and they may constructively criticise such aspects as tone, pace, and body language. The simulators provide virtual reality (VR) that enables speakers to practice before a simulated audience so that they can get used to the experience and minimize the fear.

In the actual delivery, technology is extremely important. With the help of advanced presentation software, it is possible to use dynamic visual aids that can be very interesting and help to grasp the main ideas. Such interactive features as live polls and wait questions with the utilization of AI will captivate audiences in more active communication, turning a monologue into a dialogue. Not only does this interactivity keep the audience interested, but it also gives the speaker direct feedback and thus he/she can adjust accordingly on the spot.

On top of the stage, technology lends itself to expanding public speaking on the digital platform. Virtual conferencing and live streaming technologies are technologies that help speakers communicate with distant communities around the world without having to face any geographical limitations. Social networks provide a medium through which the audience can further interact and discuss what the speaker has said and share the fact that there is a community behind the message of the speaker.

The issue of the ethics of AI in public speeches cannot be disregarded. Although AI has many advantages, concerning originality and authenticity, it creates issues of authenticity and originality. AI-simulated content should not be treated as the dominating factor in terms of audience association with the speaker because the speaker should be allowed to have a personal voice and point of view in order to ensure a genuine connection. To maintain credibility and trust, transparency concerning the system of applying AI to creating content should be a must.

On the whole, the impact of AI and technology on current-day public speaking is versatile. It gives a better chance for the speaker to deliver his or her messages as convincingly and powerfully, besides compelling him or her to give the implications a lot of consideration. With ongoing technological advances, speakers are also advised to use their potential with due responsibility, not to ruin the effectiveness of their messages due to technological abuse. With the due integration of AI and technology, a public speaker can only become more proficient and capable of delivering his/her words by involving and inspiring people in a way that has never been possible.

VIRTUAL AND HYBRID SPEAKING

In contemporary practice of public speaking, the development of technology has also created a new epoch in which the physical space is overcome by digital communication. Two new variants of communication have emerged, exist side by side, and interrelate with each other as a result of this change: virtual communication and hybrid speaking. Both of them offer their opportunities and challenges to take care of, requiring speakers to make use of them differently.

What seemed like a technology used by fringe technology enthusiasts, Virtual speaking has become a common part of the arsenal of modern orators. It is characterized by the assumption of giving the speech/speech, presentations, or lectures purely online and having the audience in different places. Lack of a physical audience places the speakers in a position to utilize the means of keeping people interested. In this case, the screen becomes a border and a connection, and speakers have to use the strength of visualisation, speech liveliness, and interactivity in order to impress their listeners.

The inability to receive instant feedback is one of the main weaknesses of virtual speaking. Lack of non-verbal representations of feelings, like nods and smiles, means one should raise their consciousness to their expressive capabilities. Presenters have to be skillful in reading the digital cues, the volume of comments in the chat box, or the number of members that come in and out of a conference to understand the feedback of the audience on their presentation. This is an art that needs a combination of intuition and technical expertise, where the presenter has to merge answers and the flow of the presentation smoothly.

In contrast, hybrid talking is the combination of the old and the new, so it is a mixture of in-person and virtual interactions. It is a form that is gaining popularity in conferences, seminars, and in corporate gatherings where part of the audience is present physically, whereas others are remote. There is a dual nature of hybrid speaking where the speaker has to cater to both groups of audiences at the same time and not leave anyone feeling left out.

When the speaker manages to switch between communicating with both in-person and virtual participants, it is essential to have such an experience in a hybrid environment. Some of these techniques include direct eye contact with the camera, pausing at strategic moments to enable one to interact virtually, and including language, which is crucial. Also, interaction with the use of technology can be provided, i.e., through the polls, Q&A, and live feedback tools to make the interaction as comfortable as possible for all participants.

Virtual and hybrid speaking needs great preparation and rehearsal. The most important one is to be acquainted with the technology used, as the technical issue may affect the continuity and credibility of the speaker. Training with live configuration, be it webcams, microphones, or virtual meeting applications, can help the speaker concentrate on what to say and not the technological failure during the live event.

Public speaking has also been democratized by the emergence of virtual and hybrid speaking, which has enabled voices of various geographical and cultural origins to be heard in global discussions. This diversity of opinions broadens the horizon of thinking and makes the conversation more enriching, as public speaking is less of a one-sided thing.

Since the world of a speech on stage is still developing, skills navigating the virtual and hybrid environments would also turn into a defining ability of a modern speaker. A thorough comprehension of these formats can not only broaden the outreach of any speaker, but also improve his or her capacity to connect, inspire, and bring change in the now more connected world.

ADAPTING TO CHANGE

The art of the speech is closely connected with the skill of reaching the audience, and this skill requires flexibility and a sense of the ever-changing environment of modern communication. The world continues to change, and this means that the methods and tactics that public speakers use must change as well, and there must be a flexible way of thinking that will manage to ride the vast seas of change.

In this era of rapid change, different forms of change occur through technological change and cultural change, among others, and each comes with its challenges and opportunities. In my opinion, the speakers should learn how to comprehend these changes and incorporate them into their presentations so that they can still sound topical and meaningful. This cannot be handled at a superficial level; there must be a greater insight into the audience's perception and involvement in the change of these measures.

The technological innovation has transformed communication, and it has provided us with tools that were inconceivable decades ago. The development of digital platforms, social media, and multimedia presentations has given speakers more options to communicate with their audiences. It also, however, requires the speakers to be technically savvy to help them use these tools. It encompasses learning to create virtual presentations where there is no real audience, due to which speakers are limited and the need to create a similarity and make it take a screen.

In addition, the cultural environment is ever changing, with the norms and values within the society changing at a very fast pace. As a public speaker, one must be sensitive to such changes, and the content they deliver should therefore be sensitive to the points of view of various people. This requires a lot of thought about the language and tone, as well as the content, so as not to give rise to any stereotypes and prejudices that can insult the different sections of the audience. Cultural competence and inclusivity turn into the essential elements of the speaker's toolkit as these two persuasive techniques enable one to appeal to a multicultural audience that is growing in diversity.

Also, flexibility is applicable to the speaker in terms of his delivery and style. In the Lecture, the authoritative style is getting way too conversational and interactive. The audiences nowadays thirst to be engaged and prefer not receiving information on average but being a participant in a conversation. This paradigm requires the speakers to acquire the skills of telling stories, humor, and conversational skills to make the conversation dynamic, so that it is impressive and motivating.

Another crucial strategy that public speakers should employ is readiness to answer the unexpected, including technical failures, hard questions, and events they have not planned. Being able to improvise and think on one's feet is also a mark of a good speaker, having composure and control over the situation. Such flexibility additionally makes the speaker more credible, and it can develop trust in the audience because people enjoy being open and honest when it comes to difficulties.

The only thing that remains constant in this constantly changing world is change itself. With this reality, public speakers who are ready to learn how to adjust to it are bound not only to survive but thrive in the modern arena. Through information, flexibility, and by constantly practicing the art of being a good speaker, the speaker may rely on having the message heard to impact the audience forever, especially in a world that is growing much more complex.